PENTAGON PRESS

COMMITTED TO SERVE THE ARMED FORCES

THE DYNAMICS OF A POST-SOVIET SPACE

Protest and its Aftermath in Ukraine

THE DYNAMICS OF A POST-SOVIET SPACE

Protest and its Aftermath in Ukraine

Edited by

Suchandana Chatterjee

MAULANA ABUL KALAM AZAD INSTITUTE OF ASIAN STUDIES
KOLKATA

PENTAGON PRESS

The Dynamics of a Post-Soviet Space: Protest and its Aftermath in Ukraine

Edited by: Suchandana Chatterjee

ISBN 978-81-8274-921-4

First Published in 2016

Published by
PENTAGON PRESS
206, Peacock Lane, Shahpur Jat,
New Delhi-110049
Phones: 011-64706243, 26491568
Telefax: 011-26490600
email: rajan@pentagonpress.in
website: www.pentagonpress.in

Printed at Avantika Printers Private Limited.

Contents

Preface

Ukraine: Changing Storyline

Since the Maidan demonstrations in Kiev in November 2013, the events unfolded in manifold directions to reveal complex choices not only about Ukraine's political future but also about post-Cold War international relations. Till early 2014, the concern was about a home-grown turmoil: that Ukraine was facing a split between Russian-speaking regions, which included President Yanukovich's home area in the east, and the Ukrainian-speaking west. An externally-aided protest movement heralded the dawn of a new Ukraine which seemed to be receptive to an outspoken and more expressive civil society. What was understated at that point of time was President Yanukovich's inability to address the deep divide that drew the oligarchs of Ukraine away from the rest of the civil society.

Gradually, what surfaced was a saga of external intervention —not just by Russia and Russia-backers in Crimea but also by an interim government that was backed by European officials. Since Yanukovich's dramatic abdication in February 2014, there have been several turning points that culminated in 'new politics in Ukraine with lot of civic initiatives'. Experts and commentators profiled the 'strength' of the opposition that was factored on EU integration (outlined in the Association Agreement). Forebodings of a civil war situation spelt doom for the CIS space. An uncertain scenario completely beyond Yanukovich's control prepared the ground for his abdication and Russia's intervention.

The spotlight shifted from the political scenario in Ukraine to Russia's policy shift in the entire region. By early 2014—it was fairly well established that Putin was unlikely to acquiesce to the West's ulterior motive of depriving him of Ukraine's membership in his model of Eurasian Union. So, instead of propping up Ukraine as a potential team member of Eurasian Economic Union, Russia took an aggressive stance (a) by underlining a historical connection between Kieven Rus and Russia which Ukraine's new leaders failed to honour and (b) by alleging independent Ukraine as the defaulter of Gazprom gas deals. Another method was sheer display of naval force in Ukraine's western sector. An overwhelming situation emerged with Crimea as the hot seat of what appeared to be a Russia-Ukraine tussle over Sevastopol on the Black Sea where Russian fleet was stationed. Russian military intervention in Crimea took place followed by a referendum that decided the fate of Crimea in particular and of Ukraine as a whole. Amidst Putinian formulae of people's will to secede from Ukraine and people's choice to be integrated with the Russian Union, an accession treaty was signed with Crimea. Putin's entry into the Ukrainian scene punched a hole into Ukraine's sovereign status. The country was now steeped in a financial crisis. Ukraine's loss was Russia's gain: the latter now had the advantage of challenging a west-staged coup that had unsettled Putin's visions of a broad-based Eurasian Economic Union.

Many saw this as a resurrection of the Cold War. With the diabolical urge to teach the West's competitor Putin a lesson, economic sanctions were imposed on Russia mainly to choke Russian oil markets, freezing assets and banning travel. President Putin on his part demonstrated his skills to tackle the West—not just by quelling the demonstrators in Kiev, taking control of the Black Sea Fleet that was situated in the heart of the Crimean peninsula and allowing his pro-Russian gunmen to flex muscles on the eastern borders of Ukraine but also by enforcing a referendum in Crimea toying with the idea of people's choice.

Since then, a new storyline has taken shape. The West's position was to 'de-escalate' tensions in Ukraine and safeguard her territorial integrity through restrictive measures and economic sanctions related to oil and defense and banking sectors. Russia's position was to ban EU dairy product exports to the country. Putin's battlefield calculus has increased his popularity in his native country. The big question is whether sanctions are working at all, even a year after Ukraine's crisis. Ukraine matters least so far sanctions are concerned: Russians of Moscow are increasingly becoming anti-American and holding the West responsible for what the Russians of Russia are facing today: the dwindling of Russian economy and sharp fall in living standards.

Ukraine's present dispensation seems to be reform-oriented. But citizens are not too hopeful about this change in image. There is still a lot of skepticism about what can be attained. What has been glossed over time and again is the onset of civil society activism. On the face of it, the Maidan events seem to represent the people's psyche and an ethos. These twin features seem to signal the birth of a new chapter in Ukraine's political culture. But, one cannot predict whether this ethos will help to save Ukraine from further intervention and encroachments. One must not forget that since the Maidan events, Ukraine's demonstrators have remained at the backstage while their successors mentored by the authorities of the European Union have taken charge of affairs. The country has been grappling with an added fear: that of aggression of separatists from the east. Factionalism in Ukraine has not ended. The West too appears to be a divided house in taking a decision on the next course of action. The worst casualty is Ukraine itself: western norms of democracy have failed here too.

This volume is the product of some of these discussions that were initiated by participants of the symposium *Ukraine: Protest and Its Aftermath*. The event was organized on 27 November 2014 by Maulana Abul Kalam Azad Institute of Asian Studies as part of its annual seminar and symposium series on Eurasia. The idea was to bring to the table a larger spectrum of ideas about Ukraine as a game-changer in global politics. The question that has been addressed in the volume is not merely the political impasse in Ukraine and how Kiev and anti-Kiev forces were pitted against one another or whether the Maidan protests have had a lingering effect in Eurasia. The purpose here is to understand the geopolitical dynamics of a post-Soviet space.

Editor

e-mail: suchandana2008@gmail.com; suchandanachatterjee@hotmail.com

Contributors

Nandan Unnikrishnan, Vice President and Senior Fellow, Observer Research Foundation, New Delhi. E-mail: *nandan@orfonline.org*

Yury V. Dubovoy, Vice Consul and Director, Russian Centre of Science and Culture, Kolkata. E-mail: *gorky_sadan@mail.ru*

Debidatta Aurobinda Mahapatra, Department of Conflict Resolution, Human Security and Global Governance, University of Massachussetts, Boston. E-mail: *arvind.mahapatra@gmail.com*

Olexey Haran, Professor, University of Kyiv Mohyla Academy. E-mail: *haranov@gmail.com*

Premen Addy, Educationist based in Kolkata. Formerly Visiting Tutor at the Department of History and Politics, Kellog College University of Oxford, 1988-2010. E-mail: *drpremenaddy@googlemail.com*

Ajay Kamalakaran, Consulting Editor, *Russia Beyond the Headlines* (RBTH) Asia. E-mail: *ajay.voyager@gmail.com*

Asel Murzakulova, Associate Professor, Bishkek Humanities University, Bishkek, Kyrgyzstan. E-mail: *aselmurza@gmail.com*

Introduction

Geopolitics After the Ukraine Crisis

Nandan Unnikrishnan

Relations between Russia and the West were never cordial since the end of the Cold War. Several attempts at rapprochement have been made, but with little success. But, with Ukraine, it seems that an irreparable breach has come between the West and Russia. This situation has come about because Russia and the West have been unable to arrive at a mutually acceptable accommodation at end of the Cold War.[1]

The West's refusal to treat Russia as an equal, its failure to integrate Moscow into the Western order on reasonable terms and the Kremlin's clamour for a multi-polar world reflecting its refusal to accept a US dominated world, has only added to the antagonism. The Ukraine crisis has brought back the spectre of great power politics, ended the post-Cold War status quo in Europe, and heightened rivalry between the two sides.[2] Today the conflict is not ideological; it is geopolitics at its worst.

While Russia concentrates on consolidating integration in the former Soviet space, the US wants to restore a holding line against Russia in Europe.[3] The conflict is thus a consequence of the structural tension between the EU and NATO's eastward expansion and Moscow's determination to restore its traditional sphere of influence in the 'near abroad'.[4] The crisis appears to have weakened Russia (particularly if one takes into account the economic effect of the crash of oil prices that occurred virtually simultaneously with the imposition of Western sanctions on Russia), united Europe, and re-energised NATO. It has bolstered support for the US in Germany and France where anti-Americanism had been on the rise. It has made Beijing more welcome in Central Asia, which is a key part of its Belt Road Initiative. Beijing also benefits because Washington is distracted – focussing on the security needs of its European allies, rather than its "pivot to Asia".[5] It is also getting energy supplies in larger quantities from Russia at lower prices. The conclusion of the gas deals with China, while long in negotiation, were partially expedited due to the Ukraine crisis as Russia felt the need to show that it had alternatives if Europe chose to decrease gas deliveries.[6]

In this whole imbroglio, Russia appears to have lost a lot and gained some. First, Russia is considerably weaker economically because of the Western sanctions as well as falling energy prices. Second, it has lost an enormous amount of soft power because it appears to have lost the propaganda battle to the West. One must recall that the Ukraine crisis happened at a time when Russia had made a comeback into world politics with its intervention in Syria to defuse the crisis between the US and Syria over the use of chemical weapons and initiating talks with Iran. However, Russia has regained its primacy in the Black Sea area as well as its ability to project power even in the Eastern Mediterranean.

The subsequent dramatic Russian intervention in the Syrian crisis has substantially altered the geo-political scenario, but does not fundamentally alter the trends in Russian economy. It bears noting that this symposium occurred well before the Russian military activities in Syria. This, naturally, reflects in the papers assembled in this volume. The symposium did not focus much on the effect of the Ukraine crisis on India and its neighbourhood. This is an attempt to briefly address that aspect. Also, this encapsulation will attempt to reflect the views of the current political and economic elites that determine India's policies.

The Ukraine crisis presented India with several dilemmas. India found itself in the tough position of having to choose between two friendly countries and had to therefore deal with pressure from both sides – Russia and the Western world supportive of Ukraine.

It is a difficult choice for India which is at a stage in its development where it requires help, namely investments and technology, from both the US and Russia. India has good relations with the US because of shared concerns and interests in, the now popular description, the Indo-Pacific, and concerns about managing China's rise, particularly given its aggressive behaviour in the South China Sea where India also has some commercial interests. Second, there is a huge Indian Diaspora in the US and there are over a 100,000 Indian students in the US. Third, India has a $100 billion trade with the US, including in defence supplies. The US is becoming one of India's major arms suppliers. Similarly, India has a long, multi-faceted, and trusted relationship with Russia, which is India's largest defence supplier. So having to choose between the two was never going to be easy for India.

Nevertheless, so far, India has managed to balance between the two. In fact, President Putin publicly praised India along with China for their "restraint" during the Ukraine crisis. India has neither endorsed nor publicly condemned the annexation of Crimea. India has also not imposed sanctions on Russia as it has always been opposed to non-United Nations sanctions. India also believes that coercive measures are unlikely to help resolve differences among large states.[7]

Western attempts to isolate Russia and the need for Russia to find markets for its energy and defence supplies, get investments to modernize its economy and a shared desire not to have a US - dominated world is pushing Russia closer to China. This is a geopolitical nightmare for India, which has depended on Russia for decades now to balance China. In fact, the blossoming of Indo-Soviet friendship coincided with the India-China war and the Sino-Soviet rift. India's fears are heightened by what appears to be Russia breaching some unwritten understandings. Chief among them is the understanding that Russia will not supply

China defence technology that is equal to or higher than what is bought by India.

New Delhi is also concerned about the growing overtures between Russia and Pakistan, with some Indian analysts believing that China has some role in prodding the two countries to come closer. India worries that when the sanctions really bite Russia, it will have no choice but to sell arms to both China and Pakistan. This, in some ways, will have the unintended effect of pushing India closer to the US.

Third, the crisis raised several questions, academic and otherwise, for India. For instance, there is the question of territorial integrity versus the right to self-determination and the right to secede. India has a long-standing opposition to breaking up existing territorial states in the name of self-determination. Given that secessionist movements have confronted India since independence, New Delhi has been an unwavering champion of the territorial integrity of states.[8] (Bangladesh being an exception). Pakistan does not view the conflict as a territorial dispute with India but calls it a matter of self-determination for the people of Kashmir.[9] The situation in Ukraine immediately reminded Indian policymakers and analysts of Kashmir. Though the then Indian NSA said Russia had "legitimate interests" in Crimea, India is uncomfortable with the idea of referendums held in the presence of foreign troops.

Then there is the question of territorial integrity versus the principle of non-interference in domestic affairs of other countries. India has been wary of great power intervention in the internal affairs of developing states because of 'humanitarian concerns' or the 'responsibility to protect'.[10] Despite being a democracy, India has maintained considerable distance from the post-Cold War international interventionist agenda, both unilateral and multilateral.[11] Both the West and Russia breached the principle of non-interference in Ukraine. For instance, if a protest were to take place in India and foreign diplomats were to distribute food to the protestors, India would have never have tolerated it. Therefore, clearly, what some American diplomats did was, to put it mildly, beyond the scope of their diplomatic duties. While the West may have egged on the opposition to oust President Yanukovych, the events this triggered in Eastern Ukraine could not have been possible without active and substantial Russian support to the separatists.

The latter brings up the question of how to deal with hybrid wars. This again has resonance in India because of what Pakistan has been doing in Kashmir for years. India is not comfortable with the idea of "little, green men" crossing borders. Finally, India would like a political resolution to the crisis by taking into account the legitimate interests of all parties—including those of Ukraine's minorities and neighbours.[12]

Ideally, now the best solution to the Ukraine crisis appears to be the observance of the Minsk agreements and the re-absorption of the separatist dominated parts of Eastern Ukraine into Ukraine with appropriate caveats. In addition, it may help to have a buffer zone between Russia and NATO consisting, ideally, of Belarus, Ukraine, Georgia, and Azerbaijan.[13] These countries would have no security alliances, bilateral or multilateral, that include mutual defence commitments for the buffer zone states, and no foreign troops, rotational or otherwise, on their territories.[14] However, they should be free to develop economic ties as suits them best.

This volume on '*Ukraine: Protest and its Aftermath*' contains several interesting perspectives on the Ukraine crisis from leading experts. Yury V. Dubovoy's chapter deals with instability in the region after the crisis started and how this could spill over to Europe, where there are underground militias of ultranationalist groups. Debidatta Aurobinda Mahapatra examines Rival Versions of Protests in Ukraine and their Geopolitical Implications and argues that the Ukrainian crisis is a reflection of the realist world order and its persistence. Olexiy Haran examines domestic and external factors in mass protests in Ukraine. He suggests that an effective and sustainable Ukrainian democracy is a threat to Putin's regime. This is why Putin is trying to destabilize Ukraine, especially after the annexation of Crimea and Russia's attempts to change territorial borders in the east of Ukraine. Premen Addy looks at Ukraine as the manifestation of the new Cold War between Russia and the US. In his chapter, Ajay Kamalakaran gives a Russian Perspective on the crisis in Ukraine, arguing that Washington must accept that Moscow has genuine interests and its own sphere of influence in the former Soviet space and Central Asia. Asel Murzakulova examines the narrative strategies used by different Facebook groups in Kyrgyzstan to explain their positions on Ukraine.

These perspectives have enriched the quality of this volume. I hope the volume will be of interest to policymakers and scholars alike.

ENDNOTES

1. C. Raja Mohan, 'India: The Quest for Balance in Asia', in Felix Hett and Moshe Wien (eds.) *Between Principles and Pragmatism: Perspectives on the Ukraine Crisis from Brazil, India, China and South Africa,* May 2015, p.6.
2. Dmitri Trenin, 'The Ukraine Crisis and the Resumption of Great-Power Rivalry', July 9, 2014, http://carnegie.ru/2014/07/09/ukraine-crisis-and-resumption-of-great-power-rivalry#
3. Dmitri Trenin, 'The Ukraine Crisis and the Resumption of Great-Power Rivalry', July 9, 2014, http://carnegie.ru/2014/07/09/ukraine-crisis-and-resumption-of-great-power-rivalry#
4. C. Raja Mohan, 'India: The Quest for Balance in Asia', in Felix Hett and Moshe Wien (eds.) *Between Principles and Pragmatism: Perspectives on the Ukraine Crisis from Brazil, India, China and South Africa,* May 2015, p.5.
5. Mike Eckel, 'China May Be Biggest Winner from Ukraine Crisis', 1 September 2014, http://www.voanews.com/content/china-ukraine-russia-benefits/2432373.html.
6. Björn Alexander Düben, 'Banking on Beijing: What the Ukraine Crisis Means for the Future of China-Russia Relations', *Strategic Update* 15.3, July 2015, www.lse.ac.uk/.../reports/pdf/IDEAS-SU15.3-ChinaRussia.pdf, p. 9.
7. C. Raja Mohan, 'India: The Quest for Balance in Asia', in Felix Hett and Moshe Wien (eds.) *Between Principles and Pragmatism: Perspectives on the Ukraine Crisis from Brazil, India, China and South Africa,* May 2015, p.6.
8. C. Raja Mohan, 'India: The Quest for Balance in Asia', in Felix Hett and Moshe Wien (eds.) *Between Principles and Pragmatism: Perspectives on the Ukraine Crisis from Brazil, India, China and South Africa,* May 2015, p.5.
9. C. Raja Mohan, 'India: The Quest for Balance in Asia', in Felix Hett and

Moshe Wien (eds.) *Between Principles and Pragmatism: Perspectives on the Ukraine Crisis from Brazil, India, China and South Africa,* May 2015, p.5.

10. C. Raja Mohan, 'India: The Quest for Balance in Asia', in Felix Hett and Moshe Wien (eds.) *Between Principles and Pragmatism: Perspectives on the Ukraine Crisis from Brazil, India, China and South Africa,* May 2015, p.5.
11. C. Raja Mohan, 'India: The Quest for Balance in Asia', in Felix Hett and Moshe Wien (eds.) *Between Principles and Pragmatism: Perspectives on the Ukraine Crisis from Brazil, India, China and South Africa,* May 2015, p.5.
12. C. Raja Mohan, 'India: The Quest for Balance in Asia', in Felix Hett and Moshe Wien (eds.) *Between Principles and Pragmatism: Perspectives on the Ukraine Crisis from Brazil, India, China and South Africa,* May 2015, p.5.
13. Dmitri Trenin, 'The Ukraine Crisis and the Resumption of Great-Power Rivalry', July 9, 2014, http://carnegie.ru/2014/07/09/ukraine-crisis-and-resumption-of-great-power-rivalry#
14. Dmitri Trenin, 'The Ukraine Crisis and the Resumption of Great-Power Rivalry', July 9, 2014, http://carnegie.ru/2014/07/09/ukraine-crisis-and-resumption-of-great-power-rivalry#

1

Instability in Eurasia in the Background of Current Financial, Social and Value Crisis

Yury V. Dubovoy

Today, across Eurasia, we see a series of events which have destabilized the whole continent. These events began few years ago as the "colour revolutions" in the former Soviet Union and the "Arab Spring" in the Arab world; today it has led to successive military action in different regions of Eurasia, with the risk of global conflict.

Despite the different events that have taken place in Eastern Europe (including Ukraine) and Middle East, there seem to be some common features among them. Also, they have common roots and driving forces. The common features include: devastation and destruction of the Islamic State in Iraq and Syria, the rapid spread of their adherents' worldwide, exponential growth in the loss of human lives, the appearance of recruiters in most of the European countries. The related links are the following: ultranationalist forces taking a fascist turn, mass executions of civilians, inhuman atrocities that include bombing of schools and kindergartens, along with destruction of legendary cities.

Why do we connect these two phenomena, seemingly so different? This is for a reason. It is well known that in the case of the war in Iraq and in Syria, as well as in Ukraine, there are representatives who are either supportive of the Islamists or are fighters who represent the fighting forces. In both cases, they are representatives of various countries and people from all over the world.

During last few decades, there has been a debate about "postmodern culture" and its expanded conceptual boundaries. Apparently simple concepts such as "terrorism", "separatism", "totalitarianism", "democracy", "freedom", "dictatorship" were developed in ways that brought about a wide range of meanings that redefined the "friend – enemy" label. Using the contemporary notions about democracy and freedom as the highest moral it is impossible to understand all the processes that are taking place in different parts of the world, even in Ukraine. Why has Yanukovych regime in Ukraine had fallen to the twenty-thirty-forty thousands of people (from 140 million population of Ukraine), gathered in the centre of Kiev? Why do people, who yesterday considered residents of other regions of the country as their fellow citizens, now advance to kill them with all kinds of weapons? Why today the rebel region of Ukraine are protected not only by their citizens, but also volunteers from France, Germany, Italy and the Scandinavian countries, despite the official position of the leadership of these countries and one-sided propaganda of the Western media? And also why the Iraq army actually did not resist the offensive of the Islamic State? Why Islamic state recruiting so many Europeans for them in France, Germany, the Scandinavian countries (not "new citizens", but the native Europeans) and how do you convince the liberal Europeans to die for a religious cause or in combat or be the suicidal terrorist with explosives who does not hesitate to blow himself up at a public place? The answers to all these questions are both simple and complicated.

Let us dwell on the situation in Ukraine and Eastern Europe. Recent activities of the ultranationalists in Germany, Poland and some other countries suggest that Ukraine is not unique in the European space. And this situation in Ukraine has a chance to spread to neighbouring countries. Let me briefly note a number of the causes of these phenomena, before I dwell on some of them. These reasons are transnational and global. Significant among them are:

1. Exhaustion of liberal ideas as the engine of social progress. Discrediting of the institutions of Western democracy and values of postmodern society in the eyes of the younger generation.
2. The ongoing financial crisis and rapidly increasing financial stratification of society in different countries.
3. The presence of unresolved territorial disputes which do not reflect the ethnic, cultural and historical realities in Europe and the Middle East.
4. Lack of a modern constructive concept, maybe we can call it "new positive ideology", which is capable of uniting representatives of different nationalities and cultures in the name of progress.

Of course, there are other reasons too.

Now some more details. After the collapse of the Soviet Union the bipolar world ceased to exist. Subsequent events have clearly demonstrated that the deterrent on both sides was not only the negative factor, such as the arms race, forcing ideological passions, mutual dislike of the two systems, but also the positive factor, characterized by constructive competition. In an effort to become popular both systems improved their quality of life. What methods and resources were used for this purpose is more a topic of discussion among economists. The basic fact is that with the Soviet collapse, unipolar rivalry ended. But, as we know from the basic law of economics, full-scale development is impossible without competition. That is why after the disintegration of the Soviet Union and the destruction of the "socialist bloc" some processes had begun, which are now so unpopular among young people and conservative circles – denial of traditional family values, material wealth, tolerance in the form of subordination of the interests of the majority to the minority, the lack of answers to the questions about higher destiny of man, etc. How can the young people respond to these challenges? As usual, they are the concentrated force and represents the energy of protest, which may increase and can evolve in any direction at any time. For example, it can be directed against some political regimes or countries.

The impact of global financial crisis of 2008 is still continuing. It is clear today that the middle class, which appeared in the West by the policy of unrestrained consumer credit, with the strengthening of this crisis will inevitably suffer losses, creating a favourable environment for the development of all kinds of protests. This middle class comprises of educated people and their children, who have a balanced standard of living. The natural decline in living standards of these people will create an environment of protest. This, in conjunction with corrupt practices dominant in many leading countries, created the ground for social unrest.

The increase in corruption, along with a sharp drop in living standards (all of us remember the golden loaves and bowls in President Yanukovych's country house in Mezhigorieat the background of the rapid growth of prices and wage cuts of the salaries) triggered protests that led to the events on the Maidan. And only then the ultranationalists and members of "Right Sector" with fascist slogans had joined, and the golden loaves of the representatives of Ukrainian elite have been declared as the fault of the north-eastern neighbour – Russia.

The third point seems to be one of the most important, because any conflict always has its historical background. Let us turn to the history of borders in Eastern Europe and the Middle East, which appeared as a result of the collapse of four global empires – German, Austro-Hungarian, Ottoman and Russian – in the early 20th century. As a result in the Middle East had appeared a lot of quasi-independent Arab monarchies under the British and the French protectorate (Iraq,

Syria, Lebanon, Jordan, Saudi Arabia, Kuwait and many others). All of these were the wreckage of the Ottoman Empire, the last global Islamist state. The boundaries of the new countries have been conducted without any regard to the ethnic and religious specifics of the region. We are witness to the results of these decisions.

The same was true for Eastern Europe. As a result of the collapse of the three continental European empires almost all the countries of Eastern Europe gained its independence, many areas have been redrawn again. Ukraine is among them. It is well known that Ukraine today consists of various historical areas with civic population belonging to different ethnic origins and dominant cultures. The recognition of Ukraine as a mono-ethnic country has had serious repercussions.

Let us see the constituent historical parts of Ukraine. It is necessary to start with the central region. This includes the Kiev land, Podolia and Slobodan Ukraine – with some modifications, the same land, which were combined with Russian Tsarist regions as a result of the decisions of the Ukrainian Hetman Bogdan Khmelnitsky and his Council in the 17th century. Before this act this land was disintegrated due to the raids of Crimean Tatars on the one hand and the genocide of Polish landlords on the other. The people of these lands for centuries tried to survive in these cruel situations till its all-Russian and Orthodox Christian identity in the middle of the 20th century. From 13th century these lands were officially known in Western and Byzantine chronicles as Russia Minor, i.e. "Little Russia".

The second region is Novorossia that is "New Russia". This term today in the light of the civil war in Ukraine has more political rather than historical meaning. In the historical sense – this is the land from Kharkov to Odessa, i.e. almost the entire northern Black Sea region, (including Donbass and Crimean peninsula) which Russia overran in the 17th–18th centuries during the wars with the Ottoman Empire. These lands were later reconquered by the multi-ethnic people of the Russian Empire – Russians, Greeks, Armenians, Malorussians (as Ukrainians called themselves till 20th century), Kalmyks, Moldovans and other peoples. This alliance of peoples throughout all the 20th century retained its all-Russian and Orthodox identity, native language of this land was Russian and only formally it belonged to Ukraine in accordance with the administrative borders of the USSR conducted by Vladimir Lenin in the 20th century. It was one big country and this was never disputed upon.

And the third major ethno-cultural community is based in Western Ukraine. This has interesting features. Initially, the western part of ancient Russia called Galicia-Volynia (center – the city of Lvov) in the 13th century, lost communication with the rest of Russian lands. For centuries the region was under the rule of Lithuania, Poland and the Austro-Hungarian Empire until the middle of 20th century, when it was united with the Soviet Union. It was Stalin's decision that the land of Galicia became part of the Ukrainian Soviet Republic. Here, in the 19th–20th centuries under the Austro-Hungarian rule, was born modern Ukrainian identity, which is the image that is now being presented by the new authorities of Ukraine as the only truth. Actually, even at that time it was not that widespread—even if we do not consider the genocide on the part of Austro-Hungarian authorities of Ukrainians who called themselves "Rusyns" (the old ethnonym of Russians) and considered themselves as part of a single large entity—the Russian people. According to historians, during World War I, in the Austro-Hungarian concentration camps Thalerhof and Terezin (first in Europe, long before the camps of Hitler), about 30,000 Galicians died. In this war, a total of more than 200,000 Galicians were killed, of whom 100,000 fled to neighbouring Russian territories. Thus, by ethnic cleansing, in this region a monolithic national community was formed, which although had Russian roots, was expected to reject everything Russian because of the nationalist fervour. During World War II there were such personalities in Western Ukraine as Stepan Bandera and Roman Shukhevych, who fought with their troops on the side of Hitler. They fought their kinsmen—hundreds of thousands of lives of Russian, Ukrainians, Poles, Jews and other people (about 5.3 million people).

Bandera and Shukhevych's activities were condemned by the Nuremberg Trial and others were recognized by the international community as war criminals (these accusations are still there). These persons are the heroes of today's "post-revolutionary" Ukraine. The ideology of "westerners" as they are called in Ukraine, declared that they are identified as the only true authentic-Ukrainian. Those, who will not agree with them, are the enemies. The results of this transformation can be clearly seen in districts of Odessa (May 2, 2014), Mariupol (May 9, 2014), Slavyansk, Donetsk, Lugansk and other cities and villages. According to German intelligence sources, the real losses in the civil war in Ukraine comprise of more than 50,000 victims.

We should also need to reflect on the status of Crimea. It is believed that Crimean Tatars are the indigenous population of Crimea. However, this is not the whole story. The Tatars came to Crimea, as well as in the southern Russian steppes, only in the 13th century. Until that time Crimea, or Tauria, as it was called in those days, was the periphery of the Byzantine Empire, and it was cohabitated by the representatives of different ethnicities and cultures – Greeks, Armenians, Bulgarians, Russian, Goths, Genoese, Scythes and Cumans. Here, in 10th century, in the ancient city of Chersonesus (near modern Sevastopol), the Russian Prince Vladimir the Great was baptized and married the sister of the Byzantine emperor. After the fall of Byzantium, Crimea became an Ottoman protectorate and was rapidly Türkicized. Already in the 15th century Crimea overran all nationalities, except for the Turks and Crimean Tatars, and the peninsula became one of Europe's largest centres of slave trade. Since the end of the 15th century the Crimean Khanate, carried out repeated raids on the Russian State and Poland. The main goal of the raids was the capture of slaves and their resale to the Turkish markets. The total number of slaves who passed through the Crimean market, is estimated at three million. The Russo-Turkish War of 1768-1774 marked the end of Ottoman rule and the slave trade in Crimea. According to Küçük Kaynarca Peace Treaty in 1774 the Ottomans renounced claims to Crimea to the Russian Empire. In

Crimea descendants of Greek, German, Bulgarian, Russian and other refugees begun to return. As a result, the Crimean Tatars have become full-fledged citizens of Russia with all the ensuing rights. A little less than two centuries later, according to the decision of the then Soviet Premier Nikita Khrushchev, Crimea was transferred from Russia to Ukraine "as a sign of eternal friendship between peoples". Both republics were then the parts of the Soviet Union. Twenty three years since Ukraine's independence after Soviet collapse, the Crimeans have demanded reunification of the peninsula with Russia. These are the sentiments of the people of Crimea that have been clearly demonstrated in a referendum in March 2014, during which 96% were in favour of a shared future with Russia. The referendum in Crimea pushed for a coup in Kiev and subsequent aggression by the Ukrainian nationalists. It is not known for certain whether it was a referendum and the subsequent reunification of the Crimea with Russia that saved the peninsula from the "Donbass-case scenario" and the genocide of the local population by the neo-Nazis. During those days the slogan "Crimea is 'Ukrainian' (inhabited only by Ukrainians), or deserted" was very popular in Kiev.

Finally, let's talk about the ideological turns. Today, we see a decay of moral ideals as new superficial ideas emanating out of different ideologies have taken shape. On the one hand there is radical Islam which declares other currents within traditional Islam as infidels. Such thoughts create confusion in the realm of ideas. Researchers from The Soufan Group based in New York, mentioned that by the end of May 2014 there were 12,000 people from 81 countries who were recruited as militants. Among them 3,000 people were from the West. Today their number is probably even higher. Two years back, media reports from Pakistan indicated that a village in North Waziristan is populated by "German Taliban", where one can hear German more often than Arabic, Pashto or Urdu. The scale of involvement of "German Islamists" in Afghanistan-Pakistan region is reportedly high. The youth are the main recruits and their actions are explained by the desire of young people to seek an identity that integrates them with the Islamic East. As it turns out, many of them, at the time of departing from Europe to the Middle East to join the ranks of the Islamic State. Their aim is not to learn the basics of the faith, but about how to quickly integrate into the new environment. Such perspective indicates that the main and most attractive place for these people is not in Islam as it is, but in protest against the imposed life style of western society.

The same can be seen in Eastern Europe but in different forms. A notable example of this changed form is to be found in Ukraine. Socio-economic and cultural contradictions have made the younger generation radical in the conditions of their disengagement with the political elites and the authorities. This is a given (and is also recognized by Ukrainian ultra-nationalists themselves): throughout the period of Ukraine's independence since 1991, there were numerous youth, educational and paramilitary organizations whose activities were subordinated to a common goal – the promotion of ideas of Ukrainian nationalism and racial exclusivity. In other words, these were fantastic ideas, appreciated by young people. There seemed to be a revival of negative ideas of national superiority and hatred towards other ethnic groups (as we have seen in the 1930s in Nazi Germany). Knowledge dissemination in these quasi-military formations was conducted under the direction of descendants returning from exile – former members of the Nazi troops led by Bandera and Shukhevych. These organizations continuously recruited youth who dispersed under conditions of post-Soviet chaos and corruption. In the twenty three years that have elapsed, these organizations have become well-organized groups which played a decisive role in the protests on the Maidan in its final phase. In these organizations, as well as in the formation of Islamist bloc in the Middle East, there were built-in ideologies about the image of the enemy (state authorities and neighbouring countries). In the context of the usurpation of power by representatives of Western Ukraine (which constitutes a minority), the beginning of the civil war in the country was only a matter of time. And the formation of military blocs in other regions of Ukraine, which were declared as "insufficiently patriotic", was also a matter of time. People in the Southern and Eastern Ukraine took up arms to defend their dignity and fundamental human right – the right to live. For a majority of Ukrainian oligarchs this situation was congenial from the point of view of business. "Nothing personal, it's just business".

Not expecting the invocation of humanity and moral values of the initiators of the bloody civil conflict, the militia of Southeast Ukraine has evolved in a short time to the Army of Novorossia, and strongly rebuffed the ultranationalists. Thus, the civil war situation is in the heart of Europe, i.e. in Ukraine, which has the risk to spill over into neighbouring European countries, where there are also underground militias of the ultranationalist groups. Now their representatives are fighting in the ranks of official military forces in Ukraine together with their Ukrainian peers.

Nowadays we often hear about the similarities in historical moments: in the 1930's too there was a similar situation in which similar factors resulted in the historical events: viz. economic crisis, social unrest, unresolved territorial disputes and historical blunders. It does not matter whether such interpretations are based on real facts or are figments of imagination. What matters is that radical views increased over time and resulted in various forms of protest and confrontation. How all that ended in the middle of the 20th century is well known. Today the aim of global actors should not be to prioritise their political interests and personal ambitions but unify in order to solve all problems that have now accumulated. The aim should not be to further geopolitical interests and go out of bounds —whether it is Fascism in Europe or radical Islam in the Middle East. Our own experience suggests that the prices might be too high to imagine.

BIBLIOGRAPHY

Galician Golgotha, *The War Crimes of the Habsburg Monarchy 1914-1917*– USA, Trumbull Conn. Peter S. Hardy Lane, 1964.

'Crimea, History', *Brockhaus and Efron Encyclopedic Dictionary in 86 Volumes.* Saint-Petersburg, 1890-1907.

96.77% of Crimeans in referendum voted for the reunification of Crimea with Russia as the federal subject of the Russian Federation, March 16, 2014; http://crimea.gov.ru/news/17_03_2014_3

'United Continent': European volunteers fighting Kiev troops in Eastern Ukraine // Russia Today; http://rt.com/news/183864-ukraine-european-volunteers-fighting/

Far-right rioters leave trail of destruction in Polish capital, by Marcin Goettig and Pawel Florkiewicz // Reuters; http://www.reuters.com/article/2013/11/12/us-poland-nationalists-march-idUSBRE9AA0N920131112

A.V. Storozhenko, "Malaia Rossiia ili Ukraina?" First published in 1918 in the journal *Malaia Rus*; repr. in *Ukrainskii separatism v Rossii. Ideologiia natsional'nogo raskola*, comp. M.B. Smolin (Moscow, 1998)

Sicherheitskreise: Bis zu 50.000 Tote // Frankfurter Allgemeine; http://www.faz.net/aktuell/politik/ausland/ukraine-sicherheitskreise-bis-zu-50-000-tote-13416132.html

Boris Yakemenko, *Who and what is ISIL? The response requires a rejection of the old paradigm of thinking*, 18.11.2014; http://www.odnako.org/blogs/ostriy-vopros/

Richard Barrett, *Foreign Fighters in Syria.* June 2014; http://soufangroup.com/wp-content/uploads/ 2014/06/TSG-Foreign-Fighters-in-Syria.pdf

2

Rival Versions of Protests in Ukraine and their Geopolitical Implications

Debidatta Aurobinda Mahapatra

Evaluating protests in an international theater is not an easy endeavor, and it is particularly difficult in post-Soviet space. The scholars are bewildered to decipher the Ukrainian protests and about what exactly happened on the ground when President Yanukovych left Kiev in February 2014, what are the factors that moved the protestors to the Maidan and why the international powers squabble so much over the developments. There is no unanimity among the analysts as reflected in opinion articles and media reports about the events in Ukraine. Yanukovych, who was democratically elected, insists that he was forcibly evicted from power, while his opponents claim that he left the office due to popular unrest against his policies that undermined the democratic aspirations of the people. Yanukovych insists that the protests were stage-managed by his Western detractors; his opponents deny the charge. Amidst these rival claims, Ukraine suffered, about 6000 people lost lives. The conflict is still continuing, giving rise to apprehension of the return of the Cold War in a new avatar with more dangerous consequences.

Despite Western sanctions, movement of forces by Ukraine and Russia, and several rounds of talks, the protests have continued. But the theatre has changed. Earlier, the Maidan, the capital in Kiev, was the prime location of the protests. Later, Lugansk and Slovyansk in the east became the new theatres of protest. The protests have forced change of guard in Kiev, but have not helped stabilize the country. Rather the protests have raised a larger question – are protests essentially harbingers of peace and development or are they ploys on part of powerful players to seek fulfillment of their interests? So far, as the Ukrainian protests reveal, the unrest have caused territorial disintegration, displacement and loss of lives. Regional and international organizations have failed to broker peace. Protests have in fact increased, while peace has remained elusive.

The paper examines the divergent interpretations of the Ukrainian protests. The paper analyzes some of the key events, and then explores how they are interpreted differently by the rival groups. The analysis will be mainly based on a study of media reports from the East and the West, and statements of the political leaders of Ukraine, Russia, EU and the US. It will particularly address the following questions: What is the raison d'etre of the current tumult? Who are the key players in the protests and what are their interests? What are the geopolitical implications of the conflict?

Post-Cold War Ukraine

This section briefly focuses on post-Cold War Ukraine and how Ukraine has increasingly been factored in the geopolitical calculus of the West. The Soviet Union collapsed in 1992. Along with Ukraine, 14 more new states emerged on the debris of the Union. During the initial years the West was interested in developing relations with Russia, and particularly in ensuring political and economic stability within the country. Olga Alexandrova argues that the initial response of the West towards Ukraine was characterized by negligence. She characterizes the period from 1991, the year Ukraine got independence, to 1993 as the period of "neglect and annoyance" as the West was preoccupied with Russia. According to her, "After the Soviet Union had disappeared, the earlier fixation on the USSR and Mikhail Gorbachev was uncritically transposed to Russia and Boris Yeltsin. Western policymakers considered Ukraine to be marginal and of lesser importance".

In this period of neglect, Ukraine was considered a part of "Russia's legitimate sphere of influence". Alexandrova argues, one of the major reasons behind this negligence was the young Ukrainian diplomacy did not have access to lobbies, parliamentarians and diplomats in the West. The West was also pre-occupied with prospects of proliferation of nuclear weapons in Ukraine. Leonid Kuchma, the former Ukrainian leader, observed in 1993, "On the map of world leaders, Ukraine does not even exist. They are indifferent whether Ukraine is independent or not".[2]

According to Mroz and Pavliuk, it was only after 1994, when nationalist parties like the Liberal Democratic Party of Russia of Vladimir Zhrinovsky emerged, and Russia's great power status in 'near abroad' increased, the West evinced interest in Ukraine. They argue that for security of Europe an independent Ukraine, separate from Russian influence, is crucial.[3] It was only in late part of the 1990s that the Western approach towards Ukraine changed. In September 1995, British Foreign Secretary Malcolm Rifkind called Ukraine a "strategic pivot" in the post-Cold War order.[4] Larrabee argues, "An independent Ukraine transforms the geopolitics of Europe. The reincorporation of Ukraine into Russia or a Russian-dominated security system would have a major impact on European security, bringing the shadow of Russian power back to Central European border".[5] Following the Orange Revolution in 2004, the West evinced more interest in Ukraine. There was increasing emphasis in policy circles that Ukraine's security is key to Europe's stability. Writing in 2009, Karatnycky and Motyl argued, "Ukraine must be placed back on the policy agenda, as a player in its own right, not as an afterthought to a policy toward Russia... By producing a stronger, more secure, and more stable Ukraine, the West would effectively be laying the foundations for stronger, more secure, and more stable relations with Russia.[6]

In order to understand the conflict in Ukraine and particularly how it is difficult for its leaders to adopt a pro-West or pro-Russia orientation in its foreign policy, one must factor the highly diverse character of the Ukrainian society that makes the construction of a single Ukrainian identity and a single orientation difficult. Angela Stent raised the question, "Is There a Ukrainian National Identity?" She reasoned, "Ukraine's continuing independence is contingent on forging an inclusive national identity, one that transcends ethnicity. Ukraine today is divided among its west, south, and east. Western Ukrainians consider themselves culturally, linguistically (the Ukrainian language resembles Polish more than Russian), and religiously part of Europe. Eastern and southern Ukrainians are culturally, linguistically, and religiously closer to Russia".[7] Knudson Gee argues, in order to understand the Ukrainian society and its myriad diversity one has to grasp the divisions that run deep and include such factors as nationality, language, geography, and religion. She elaborates, "West Ukraine is much more religious, and a significant number of western Ukrainians follow the historically nationalistic Uniate Church. Loyalty to the Ukrainian language and Ukrainian ethnicity are both associated with religiosity. Therefore, religious belief and affiliation may be central components of the nationalist movement in western Ukraine. Eastern Ukraine is much less religious, and those who are religious are strongly associated with the Orthodox Church"[8].

The Key Events and their Interpretations

Viktor Yanukovych ascended to power in a democratic election in 2010. The protests against his rule started towards the end of 2013. His procrastination to sign the EU Association Agreement, drafted since May 2012, furthered his image as pro-Russian, which propelled the opposition forces against him. The association agreement aimed at establishing political and economic relations between EU and Ukraine, and also entailed economic and judicial reforms on part of Ukraine to match the European standards. Yanukovych expressed willingness to join Russia-led Customs Union. Russia agreed to buy $15 billion of Ukrainian government bonds and slash price of gas it sells to the country. The protests gathered momentum in the end of 2013 after Yanukovych rejected the agreement. The protesters gathered in Maidan, the central square, in Kiev. In the beginning of the protests, it was not clear whether the West supported the protesters. However, a conversation between the US Assistant Secretary of State, Victoria Nuland and the US Ambassador to the Ukraine, Geoffrey Pyatt, leaked in early February 2014[9], indicated the increasing US interest in the change of regime in the strategic European country. Yanukovych mooted the idea of imposing emergency law to curb the protests. The Vice President of the US, Joseph Biden called Yanukovych in January 2014 to suggest to him not to declare state of emergency. According to a White House statement, Biden "underscored that the U.S. condemns the use of violence by any side, and warned that declaring a State of Emergency or enacting other harsh security measures would further inflame the situation and close the space for a peaceful resolution"[10]. In the same month, Russia called the US and the EU not to interfere in Ukraine. Later, in February 2014, Nuland and Pyatt visited the protest grounds and met the protest leaders Arseny Yatsenyuk and Vitaly Klitschko.

The developments in the region have been interpreted differently by the rival groups. The pro-West groups argue that Yanukovych was undemocratic. He stalled Ukraine's path towards the EU; hence popular protests ensued. The pro-Russia groups argue that Yanukovych was pro-Russian; hence he did not succumb to the Western pressure. His resistance to the Western pressure to abide by the terms of the EU-Ukraine agreement led to the protests. According to Robert Parry, "But Yanukovych was elected in what was regarded as a reasonably fair election in 2010. Indeed, some international observers called the election an important step toward establishing an orderly political process in Ukraine... But protesters from western Ukraine, including far-right nationalists, sought to turn this policy dispute (about Ukraine-EU Association Agreement) into a means for overthrowing the elected government… the democratically elected president was a dictator and the coup makers who overthrew the popularly chosen leader were 'pro-democracy' activists".[11]

On 21 February 2014, an agreement was brokered between President Yanukovych and the protestors. The foreign ministers of Germany, France and Poland played key roles to broker the agreement. Under the agreement, the President had to compromise his power and agree to the formation of a new national unity government. Under the agreement, the parliament had to be dissolved and new elections were to be conducted. International media captured the signing ceremony. The next day Yanukovych fled the presidential palace. What happened within the span of one day? Much of the events that transpired after the signing of the agreement and particularly on the night of 21 February remained intriguing. Much remained disputed about what transpired on that night, and about the role of various opposition groups.

The pro-West argument is that Yanukovych was unpopular. He abdicated his responsibility and fled as he could not confront the popular protests. Yanukovych deserved to be ousted from the power because he was corrupt, undemocratic and sought Russia's dominance over Ukrainian affairs. Samantha Power, the US Ambassador at the United Nations, stated at the UN Security Council: "Their (the protestors) response is reasonable, it is proportional, and frankly it is what any one of our countries would have done in the face of this threat".[12] The editorial of *Washington Post* in its 24 February 2014 edition wrote: "Ukraine has shaken off its corrupt president and the immediate prospect of domination by Russia…The moves were democratic…Kiev is now controlled by pro-Western parties that say they will implement the association agreement with the European Union that Mr. Yanukovych turned away from three months ago, triggering the political crisis".[13]

The pro-Russia and pro-Yanukovych groups argued that the President was toppled from power by the coup. Yanukovych had no option but to leave. He did not declare that he is leaving the office. He was overthrown illegally. The second version, mostly emanated from Yanukovych and his supporters including Russia, is predicated on the premise that the President was removed from power illegally. The violence that threatened his life compelled him to leave the palace, but that did not take away his power as president. According to Yanukovych, "If a president hasn't resigned, if he hasn't been impeached, and if he is alive – and you see that I am alive – then he remains the president"[14]. He further referred to the coup as a "bandit" coup[15].

It will be worthwhile to refer to the differing interpretations of the upsurge: (a) democratic and (b) banditry. While Western media and diplomats referred to the coup as a democratic upsurge, Russian media and diplomats called it illegal and constitutional, and even as 'bandit' activity. President Putin targeted the increasing Russophobia in the western part of Ukraine, particularly as practiced by the Rightist parties, and warned of a 'catastrophe' if this phobia does not stop. During his interview to Germany's ARD channel on 13 November 2014, Putin said, "we are told again and again: pro-Russian separatists must do this and this, you must influence them in this way, you must act in that way. I have always asked them: 'What have you done to influence your clients in Kiev? What have you done? Or do you only support Russophobic sentiments?' This is very dangerous, by the way. A catastrophe will happen if somebody surreptitiously supports Russophobia in Ukraine. It will be a real catastrophe!"[16]

A referendum took place in Crimea on 16 March 2014. Crimea, a constituent part of Ukraine but with majority Russian population, went into turmoil after the coup in Kiev. The Crimean parliament sought Russian help, and held a referendum on 16 March. Reports suggest that the Russian troops had entered the Crimean territory before the referendum took place. In the referendum 95.5 per cent of voters supported Crimea's secession from Ukraine and its joining to Russia[17].

The Crimean Parliament appealed Russian parliament for accession. The Russian parliament passed a resolution on 18 March, and integrated Crimea into Russian territory. The pro-West groups argue that the referendum was unconstitutional and part of Russia's imperialist design. This argument is based on the premise that the referendum and accession of Crimea to Russia was illegal, and even imperialistic. Hilary Clinton, former Secretary of State of the US and Democratic Presidential candidate, compared Russia's annexation of Crimea to Hitler's invasion of neighbors. According to her, "Now if this (Russia's role in Ukraine) sounds familiar, it's what Hitler did back in the 1930s".[18] She further elaborated, "All the Germans that were ... the ethnic Germans, the Germans by ancestry who were in places like Czechoslovakia and Romania and other places, Hitler kept saying they're not being treated right. I must go and protect my people, and that's what's gotten everybody so nervous".[19]

Russia argues that the referendum reflected the will of the people. There is already a precedent in Kosovo, supported by the West. This argument is based on the premise that the accession of Crimea to Russia is not illegal. Culturally the peninsula was linked to Russia. It was in 1954 that then Soviet leader Nikita Khrushchev had handed over Crimea from Russia to Ukraine. From international law perspective, Russia argues that there is a clear precedent about a part of state seceding from the state without taking into account the law or resolution of the parliament of the state. Putin reflected this point of view when he stated, "Whenever I hear complaints about Russia violating international law I am simply amazed. What is international law? It is first of all the United Nations Charter, international practice and its interpretation by relevant international institutions. Moreover, we have a clear recent precedent – Kosovo".[20]

On 17 July 2014, a Malaysian airplane MH 17, flying from Amsterdam to Kuala Lumpur, was shot down by a missile over the east Ukrainian airspace. All the 298 passengers including the crew died. A Dutch investigation found that the airplane was shot down by surface-to-air missile or by another aircraft. The new Ukrainian government and Russia traded charges against each other for the tragedy. There is no conclusive evidence as to who orchestrated the missile attack and with what motive, as the airplane was a civilian carrier. Many international investigations notwithstanding the real cause behind the attack, and the identification of the real culprit remain a mystery. According to pro-West interpretation, Russia supported rebels shot down the plane to portray Ukraine in poor light and its airspace as dangerous. The new government in Ukraine accused Russian hand behind the attack, which Russia denied. Russia argued that it has no hand in the incident and Ukraine is hiding the truth and blaming Russia to garner international support. The contrasting positions of the conflicting parties reveal the simplistic logic they adhere in interpreting the developments in the conflict. This simplistic logic, or this simplistic prism of friend versus foe, has sharpened geopolitical contours of the conflict.

Geopolitical Implications

The ongoing Ukrainian conflict has far reaching geopolitical implications that transcend the borders of Ukraine. Some scholars see in the conflict the premonitions of a new Cold War between Russia and the US. The American scholar, Noam Chomsky, while analyzing the violent fall outs of the Ukrainian conflict, argued, "The worst-case scenario, of course, would be a nuclear war, which would be terrible".[21] According to Russia's nationalist leader, Vladimir Zhirinovsky, "Through its current actions Ukraine is leading Europe towards a Third World War. Unfortunately, it is going to happen, and Ukraine is an instigator of this Third World War".[22]

The leaders of Russia and the US, and their allies, have already started diplomatic maneuvers, and sharpened their attacks. The US President, Barack Obama in his speech at the UN on 24 September 2014 identified "Russian aggression in Europe" among the top three global threats, the other two being Ebola and the ISIS.[23] While speaking at the NATO summit at Brussels in the same month, he cautioned Russia, "NATO will not be complacent" (if one of its allies were attacked).[24] He further stated, "Russia's aggression against Ukraine threatens our vision of Europe that is whole, free and at peace."[25] The NATO Secretary General, speaking on the occasion, argued in a veiled reference to Russia, "Should you even think of attacking one ally, you will be facing the whole alliance".[26]

The Russian President Putin criticized the Western policy towards Ukraine and justified the Russian action in the conflict. To counter the argument that Russia is providing arms to the Ukrainian rebels in the east, he argued, "People fighting for a just cause will, in the modern world, always find arms". He also claimed that whatever Russia does is perceived negatively by the West. In his words, "When Russia starts... safeguarding people and its interests, it immediately becomes bad"[27]. He justified Russia's actions by arguing "We're stronger because we're right"[28]. He reasoned, "There is war in the East of Ukraine. The Ukrainian government is using its army and even ballistic missiles. You [the West] are silent. Do you want the Ukrainian authorities to destroy everyone there [in eastern Ukraine], all their political opponents? You want that? We do not. We will not allow [this to happen]."[29] Putin blamed the West for the deteriorating situation in Ukraine and for its attempt to raise a new 'iron curtain' against Russia. According to him, "We understand the fatality of an 'Iron Curtain' for us. We will not go down this path in any case and no one will build a wall around us. That is impossible!"[30]

The Ukrainian conflict has widened the rift between Russia and the West. The sanctions against Russia have created a deep divide not only among the two major actors but also among their people. Russia has attempted to cultivate its relations towards its east and south, particularly with emerging powers such as India and China, within the framework of a strategic triangle of RIC or the grouping of BRICS. The sanctions imposed by the US and the EU on Russia may have economic implications, but the goal – peace and stability in Ukraine –

for which they were imposed, has remained elusive. Since February 2014, despite the sanctions, the fighting between Ukrainian troops and pro-Russian rebels in east Ukraine has left more than 6,000 Ukranians dead. The sanctions have only strengthened the rigid position of Moscow and contributed to a stalemate. In the case of Russia, the policy of sanctions has not proved effective, for several reasons – a major one being that the EU and Russia complement each other and are economically intertwined; so sanctions have proved counter-productive for both Russia and Europe.

In reaction, Russia has threatened to impose sanctions on planes flying from the west over its air space. Many European airlines pass over the Russian airspace towards Asia, and any diversion will cost them about four more hours of air travel and in turn, jet fuel. Well-funded airlines such as Lufthansa are projected to lose about 1 billion Euros in three months if Russia bans its airspace. Russia's sanctions on food and agricultural products from some of the western countries have resulted in the European exporters looking to a new market for goods worth about $10 billion. Federica Mogherini, the EU High Representative for foreign affairs, argued that though the sanctions have weakened the Russian economy, the conflict on the ground is manifest. Mogherini has made a case for a political solution to the crisis.

The western sanctions targeted at the rich Russians as well as the Russian state – including travel bans, limits on technological imports and co-operation and financial borrowing restrictions for state banks – are creating the intended discomfort.[31] If they persist, they will indeed impact the Russian economy in the long term. Major Russian banks such as Sberbank, VTB, Gazprombank, Vnesheconombank and Rosselkhozbank have witnessed their share prices drop. ExxonMobil has cancelled nine planned deals out of ten with Rosneft. Exxon has stated that due to the advanced nature of the gas exploration project in Kara Sea, it will take some time for the company to wind up the project. Rosneft recently requested the Russian government for a loan of $40 billion dollars to ward off the negative impact of the sanctions. In response to sanctions, many foreign investors have withdrawn capital from Russia – some reports suggest that the Russian economy could have seen a capital flight of up to $75 billion in the first half of 2014, sending its benchmark Micex index down 7.7 per cent in 2014.

The Ukrainian crisis does not revolve around territory only. Geopolitical rivalry, clash over resources and spheres of influence have played a part in the conflict. The scale of the crisis in February 2014 is not the same as in April 2015; rather, it has conflagrated, assumed international dimension and become more violent. It has widened the chasm between Russia and the West, and propelled Russia to deepen ties with the countries to its east and south. Russia signed a landmark gas deal with China during President Putin's visit to Beijing in May 2014. During the St. Petersburg International Economic Forum in May 2014, India's ONGC and Rosneft signed an agreement on cooperation in exploitation of resources in the Arctic. To encourage new investment and boost trade, Moscow signed a pact with Beijing to trade more in ruble and yuan. In October 2014, China's Exim bank agreed to finance Russia's Vnesheconombank, VTB and Rosselkhoz banks. Similarly, India's Export-Import Bank and Russia's Vnesheconombank have started talks on an arrangement, under which loans can be facilitated for Indian and Russian companies in local currencies for bilateral investment. Sberbank, Russia's largest lender stated in November 2014, that it is about to start issuing credit guarantees in Chinese Yuan. According to the bank, "An important aspect of these transactions is that post-import financing was attracted in Chinese Yuan, which is especially relevant given the existing market environment".[32]

The ceasefires between various parties to the conflict in September 2014 and in February 2015 have increased the prospects of peace in the region. Unless the conflict is depoliticised, the sanctions will only add layers to the conflict. Means of force, whether of economic sanctions or deployment of troops, induce negative peace – the violence comes to a temporary halt but fails to address the root causes of the conflict. It is another debate whether a negative peace can be the only goal even as the conflict becomes protracted and the seeds of distrust and hatred develop deeper roots.

The developments have revoked the rivalries of the Cold War. It is difficult at present to predict whether the developments will actually lead to a new Cold War or the fiery tensions will cool down with the passage of the time. The flaring up of tensions in Ukraine's east, the sanctions and the intransigent positions of the conflicting parties do not portend that every thing will be settled down in a peaceful manner. In this context, some issues must be kept in mind while analyzing the developments in the Ukraine including separation of Crimea and its possible implications for the evolving world order.

The first and foremost thing that must be factored in the analysis is that the power dynamics among nations in the post-Cold War world is different from the Cold War world. And post-Crimea is not post-Afghanistan (of 1989). There were no such groups such as the BRICS, G-20 or SCO during the Cold War. These groups have changed the old paradigm of international policy making. During the 1980s or even early 1990s, when the Cold War was at its fag end, the countries such as India and China were not emerging powers. Now India and China, along with Russia, have formed common platforms like RIC and BRICS, and add to this equation the G-20 and SCO – the balance of power is certainly not concentrated in any one part of the world. It has diffused, or rather gravitated towards Asia with India and China as crucial players.

The shifting power dynamics and its impact on the global order is recognized by all the powers including Russia and the US, but both have used and interpreted the changing equation in different ways. For Russia, the rising groups such as BRICS, G-20 and SCO can help salvage Russia from the current crisis. The BRICS as a collective body and also its members including India, China and Brazil separately have deliberately refrained to go against Russia regarding the Ukrainian crisis. Any further distancing between Russia and the West will leave Russia with options to build closer relationship with the BRICS members.

Russia will attempt to offset the Western sanctions by developing closer relationship with these countries.

The West, led by the US, has explored options to pull India and China out from the Russian influence. The US policy makers appropriately realize that the closer relationship between the BRICS countries, particularly of India and China with Russia, will impact its policies towards Russia. Hence, one of the recent US policy maneuvers is to persuade India and China to distance Russia. One of the US officials expressed this policy in very clear terms, "We are actively working on the diplomatic side to isolate Russia and that means with countries like China and India and others".[33] Economic diplomacy will be the key in determining the efficacy of such a policy maneuver, besides the strategic considerations. The attempts on part of the Europe to diversify its energy resources (which will unlikely happen in near future due to gigantic efforts such a policy will demand and also due to mutual differences and constraints of sources) and reduce its dependency on Russia will drive Russia towards energy hungry countries India and China. Already Russia and China are deliberating for a while to establish a pipeline between the two countries. India is also interested in establishing direct pipelines from Russia and in transport corridors such as north-south corridor.

Conclusion

The Ukrainian crisis and its far reaching implications bring forth the perennial debate in international politics: Does national interest dominate global peace and security? Are national interest and global peace and security diametrically opposite or complementary? These questions bring to focus the arguments to two major contending theories of international politics – realism and liberalism. In a realist world order, the states act in an anarchic system governed by the rule might is right. In this anarchic system the powerful states dominate the weak states, and the states form groups and alliances to secure their interests. In a liberal world order, the states do not sacrifice their national interests, but they consider cooperation and interdependence as major tools to foster national interests. In this system, states gain from cooperation, and national interest and international peace and security do not necessarily collide.

The Ukrainian crisis is a reflection of the realist world order. Though realism reigned supreme during the Cold War days, it seems its appeal to the states, particularly the powerful ones, is still dominant. As discussed in the first section of the article, the objective developments have been interpreted by the West and Russia differently to suit their national interests. In this altar of national interests, international peace and security have become the casualties. Since the conflict took a violent turn in February 2014, thousands have lost their lives. Hence besides the economic costs of the conflict, the humanitarian costs are enormous. But the realist politics have not allowed the humanitarian voices to proliferate. Though ceasefires have been announced to diffuse the crisis, the conflict has actually turned more violent engulfing more regions in Ukraine's south and east.

In geopolitical terms, Ukraine is situated on the faultiness of influences of Russia and of the US-led West. While the non-Russian speaking people in the western parts of the country are pro-West, the Russian speaking people in the east and the south are pro-Russian. This fault line existed during the Cold War, but it remained calm as Ukraine was a part of the Soviet Union. The fault line was exposed after the end of the Cold War and subsequent collapse of the Soviet Union. While Russia considers Ukraine as a part of post-Soviet space, hence belonging to its sphere of influence, the US-led West considers Ukraine as a part of Europe, and the country needs to be rescued from the Russia's influence. The historical memories, the cultural linkages, and the divergent aspirations of the leaders further complicate the already fragile crisis.[34] The growing chasm between Russia and the West has contributed to global stalemate. The prospects of cooperation between the two to address pressing global issues such as the Islamic State, religious extremism and terrorism, climate change have gone down due to intransigent positions of both the parties to the conflict.

ENDNOTES

1. Olga Alexandrova, "Ukraine and Western Europe", Harvard Ukrainian Studies 20 (1995): 147.
2. John Edwin Mroz and Oleksandr Pavliuk, "Ukraine: Europe's Linchpin", *Foreign Affairs* 75, no. 3 (1996): 58.
3. Mroz and Pavliuk, p. 62.
4. Olga Alexandrova, "Ukraine and Western Europe"... p. 149.
5. F. Stephen Larrabee, "Ukraine's Place in European and Regional Security", *Harvard Ukrainian Studies*, 20 (1996): 249.
6. Adrian Karatnycky and Alexander J. Motyl, "The Key to Kiev: Ukraine's Security Means Europe's Stability", *Foreign Affairs* 88, no. 3, 2009, p. 120.
7. Angela Stent, "Ukraine's Fate", *World Policy Journal* 11, no. 3, 1994, p. 83.
8. Gretchen Knudson Gee, "Geography, Nationality, and Religion in Ukraine: A Research Note", *Journal for the Scientific Study of Religion* 34, no. 3, 1995, p. 389.
9. For the details of the leak see, "Ukraine crisis: Transcript of leaked Nuland-Pyatt call", 7 February 2014, http://www.bbc.com/news/world-europe-26079957
10. Richard Balmforth and Natalia Zinets, "Ukraine's Yanukovich, opposition agree to scrap some anti-protest laws", 27 January 2014. Available at http://www.reuters.com/article/2014/01/28/us-ukraine-idUSBREA0Q11420140128
11. Robert Parry, "Cheering a 'Democratic' Coup in Ukraine", 26 February 2014. http://consortiumnews.com/2014/02/26/cheering-a-democratic-coup-in-ukraine/
12. Quoted in C.J. Chivers and Noah Sneider, "Ukrainians Strike Rebel-Held City as Fighting Spreads", *The New York Times*, 2 May 2014. Also available at http://www.nytimes.com/2014/05/03/world/europe/ukraine.html?_r=0
13. "Ukraine's Next Chapter", *Washington Post*, 24 February 2014. Available at http://www.washingtonpost.com/opinions/ukraines-next-chapter/2014/02/24/a26822be-9d87-11e3-a050-dc3322a94fa7_story.html
14. "Viktor Yanukovych urges Russia to act over Ukrainian 'bandit coup'", 28 February 2014, http://www.theguardian.com/world/2014/feb/28/viktor-yanukovych-russia-ukraine-coup
15. Ibid.
16. For the full text of the interview see "Putin: 'Supporting Russophobia in Ukraine will result in catastrophe'", 16 November 2014. http://rt.com/politics/official-word/206051-putin-russophobia-ukraine-nato/
17. "Crimea referendum: Voters 'back Russia union'", 16 March 2014, http://www.bbc.com/news/world-europe-26606097

18. Philip Rucker, "Hillary Clinton says Putin's actions are like 'what Hitler did back in the '30s'", 5 March 2014. http://www.washingtonpost.com/blogs/post-politics/wp/2014/03/05/hillary-clinton-says-putins-action-are-like-what-hitler-did-back-in-the-30s/
19. Philip Rucker, 'Hillary Clinton....
20. "Putin: 'Supporting Russophobia in Ukraine will result in catastrophe'", 16 November 2014. http://rt.com/politics/official-word/206051-putin-russophobia-ukraine-nato/
21. "Chomsky: NATO is a U.S.-run intervention force", http://rt.com/shows/sophieco/202967-cold-nuclear-war-nato/
22. "Ukraine pushing Europe to WWIII – nationalist party leader", 17 November 2014, http://rt.com/politics/206239-ukraine-europe-war-zhirinovsky/
23. For the full text of Obama's speech see http://www.washingtonpost.com/politics/full-text-of-president-obamas-2014-address-to-the-united-nations-general-assembly/2014/09/24/88889e46-43f4-11e4-b437-1a7368204804_story.html
24. Stephanie Condon, "Obama: Russian aggression in Ukraine threatens a free Europe", 5 September 2014, http://www.cbsnews.com/news/obama-russian-aggression-in-ukraine-threatens-a-free-europe/
25. Stephanie Condon, 'Obama:....
26. Condon, Óbama....
27. Gabriela Baczynska, "Putin says Russia not isolated over Ukraine, blames West for frosty ties", 23 November 2014, http://www.reuters.com/article/2014/11/23/us-russia-putin-idUSKCN0J709320141123
28. Elena Holondy, "Putin: We're Stronger Than Everybody", 23 November 2014, http://www.businessinsider.in/PUTIN-Were-Stronger-Than-Everybody/articleshow/45252173.cms
29. Pavel Felgenhauer, "Ukrainian Donbas Becomes a Russian Protectorate", Eurasia Daily Monitor 11, no. 208 (20 November 2014). Available at http://www.jamestown.org/programs/edm/single/?tx_ttnews%5Btt_news%5D=43108&cHash= 6a485461dd9b95bd67376f2beb07c688#.VULpB_lViko
30. Gabriela Baczynska, "Putin says Russia not isolated over Ukraine, blames West for frosty ties", 23 November 2014, http://www.reuters.com/article/2014/11/23/us-russia-putin-idUSKCN0J709320141123
31. Analysis of the sanctions and their impact on conflict and peace in Ukraine in Debidatta Aurobinda Mahapatra, "Sanctions are a Negative Peace", 16 October 2014, http://www.gatewayhouse.in/sanctions-are-a-negative-peace/
32. Karcper Pempel, "Russia's biggest bank launches financing in Chinese yuan", 18 November 2014, http://rt.com/business/206583-sberbank-finance-chinese-yuan/

33. "US talking with India, China to isolate Russia", *Times of India*, 29 March 2014. Also available at http://timesofindia.indiatimes.com/world/us/US-talking-with-India-China-to-isolate-Russia/articleshow/32910755.cms
34. Pavel Felgenhauer, "Ukrainian Donbas Becomes a Russian Protectorate", *Eurasia Daily Monitor* 11, no. 208, 20 November 2014. Available at http://www.jamestown.org/programs/edm/single/?tx_ttnews%5Btt_news%5D=43108&cHash= 6a485461dd9b95bd67376f2beb07c688#.VULpB_lViko

3

Euromaidan and Russian Intervention: Domestic and External Factors in Mass Protests in Ukraine

Olexiy Haran

The history of mass protests in contemporary Ukraine started during *perestroika*. The Soviet-time dissidents and new protesters joined their forces in the *Rukh* movement modeled on Lithuanian *Sajudis* and other Baltic popular fronts (*Rukh* and *Sajudis* mean the same: "Movement"). *Rukh* played an important role in Ukraine's peaceful transition to independence. It stressed importance of ethnic dialogue and tolerance, thus avoiding ethnic conflicts as in the Caucasus and Yugoslavia. The 2004 Orange Revolution was also non-violent and the Euromaidan of winter 2013-14 was non-violent for more than two months unless the first protesters were shot. Despite some stereotypes depicting Euromaidan as 'the Western plot', this movement (as previously the Orange Revolution) was the result primarily of domestic factors. After corrupt president Viktor Yanukovych left the country, transition of power to new regime was quite smooth. However, Russian annexation of Crimea and its continued intervention changed the situation. As a result, Donbas (two eastern regions of the country) sank into violence.

Background: 'Inclusive' Ukrainian Nation-building

Under the Soviet regime, Ukrainians, Jews, Crimean Tatars were subjected to Russification and national and religious discrimination. Dissidents of different nationalities experienced real, not Soviet, internationalism in Soviet prison camps. Poland's "Solidarity" movement influenced Ukraine's aspirations for independence and supported the creation in 1989 of the Ukrainian national-democratic movement *Rukh*, which in turn appealed to Ukraine's different ethnic groups to support mutual national revival. Therefore, modern Ukrainian nationalism is a territorial not an ethnic one and "inclusive" rather than "exclusive." The tolerant position of the national-democrats towards national minorities influenced the so called national-communists, who were led by independent Ukraine's first president, Leonid Kravchuk (1991-94).

In its preamble, Ukraine's 1996 Constitution defined "the Ukrainian people" as "citizens of Ukraine of all nationalities." Ukraine's independence elevated the status of what had previously been a provincial elite and became one of the values for the political and business elites whatever language they speak.

Although a law passed in 1989 proclaimed Ukrainian as the only official state language, Russian continued to play an important role in the country. The number of ethnic Russians comprises around 17 percent. But the number of those who consider Russian as their "mother tongue" is higher – almost 1/3.[1]

Is there discrimination of the Russian language? Towards the end of the Soviet regime, in 1990, only 45 percent of pupils studied in Ukrainian, and in higher education about 90 percent of subjects were taught in Russian. In independent Ukraine, the Russification of education has been halted. Nevertheless, combined number of those pupils who *study in Russian* and those who *study the Russian language as a subject* reaches almost 1/2.

About 40 percent of all books in circulation are in Russian and two-thirds of the country's newspapers are in the Russian language. Many TV and radio programmes in Ukraine are still conducted in Russian or in both languages. Due to spatial contact with Russia, young Ukrainians know the Russian language by default. Ethno-linguistic boundaries within Ukraine are blurred, and the Russian and Ukrainian languages are closely related. In fact, the very idea of a distinction between Russian- and Ukrainian-language speakers is rather exaggerated because most of the population is bilingual.[2]

Independent Ukraine has faced the challenge of nation-building by opting not only for democracy and market economy but also state institutions, and "quadruple transition". It makes the situation more difficult compared to Poland, Hungary, and the Baltic countries, a fact which has quite often been overlooked. However, because of its inclusive policy, compared to the Balkans, Caucasus and Russia, Ukraine has been able to avoid ethnic conflicts till 2014.

Maidan-I: The non-violent Orange Revolution

The 2004 Orange Revolution was a challenge to the alleged forgery during elections. The event was preceded by Georgia's "Rose Revolution". However, it was a domestic phenomenon and the Ukrainian opposition held the authoritarian Ukrainian President Leonid Kuchma responsible for the failure of the 2001 protests and the violence that erupted. Hence, the decision was to adhere to non-violent methods, similar to the ideas of Mahatma Gandhi and Martin Luther King.

Previously, the post-Soviet space was viewed by many policy-makers as a sphere of Russian influence, where post-Soviet, anti-Western political culture is dominant which restricts mobility and migration to Europe. However, that did not deter several thousands of Ukrainians to stand in freezing winter temperatures at Kyiv's central square-Maidan. It prevented authoritarian president Kuchma to bring to office its chosen candidate (Viktor Yanukovych) and, in this way, to repeat the "Yeltsin–Putin scenario". The revolution was non-violent, the participants demonstrated a high level of inter-ethnic and inter-confessional tolerance. Democratic movements in Belarus, Kenya, Taiwan and Lebanon made a reference to the successful Orange Revolution.

The Orange Revolution was described by Kremlin as 'a Western plot', which did not correspond to reality. The West's continuous support of civil society during Ukrainian independence was extremely important for its development in 1990s, but the dominant factors of the Orange Revolution were domestic. The main factors leading to the success were:

- activity of civil society which, with international support, managed to monitor the election process;
- support from small and medium-sized businesses;
- creation of broad oppositional front which used non-violent tactics;
- addressing issues of social justice helped to overcome polarizing strategy of the Kuchma regime and anti-Western propaganda;
- split within large business groups dissatisfied with Kuchma's growing authoritarianism which was used by opposition and international community to weaken Kuchma's regime;
- international criticism of the falsifications and the West's demand that Kuchma renounce the use of force;
- round table between representatives of the EU and Russia with OSCE mediation.

The main achievements of the Orange Revolution were: political freedom, (including freedom of the press) and free and fair elections.[3]

However, the Orange Revolution ended in a compromise. The 2004 constitutional reform in Ukraine created a new pattern according to European norms: the prime minister would have to rely on a parliamentary majority and the president could not remove him/her as it happened in the past. This was something that had been demanded by democratic groups for many years. On the other hand, the reform process was hectic and inconsistent. The president and prime ministers were trying to secure for themselves separate and parallel structures of power.

Compromise restricts the path of radical reforms Unlike Georgia, the struggle against corruption or judicial reform never started.

After the victory, broadbased opposition to the *ancien regime* fizzled out. Politics in Ukraine became populist, and the Orange forces became hostages of electoral democracy. The opportunity for reforms under the Orange government was lost. It had dramatic consequences after the Orange forces lost 2010 presidential elections.

The paradox is that Yanukovych also benefitted from democratic freedoms, especially free access to media. He strengthened his position by exploiting the populist opposition, which was a convenient strategy at the time of economic crisis of 2008-09.

Subsequent developments showed how fragile the gains of a young democracy could be if the positive changes enacted after the revolution are not institutionalized. The Constitutional Court faced pressure from the new President: in September 2010 it restored the 1996 version of the Constitution, therefore giving to Yanukovych all control that Kuchma had.

Euromaidan or 'Revolution of Dignity'

Mass protests in Maidan, the central square of Kyiv, during the bitter cold winter of 2013-14, known as *Euromaidan* or '*Revolution of Dignity*' were non-violent for more than two months. The demonstrations began when, under Russian pressure, President Yanukovych abruptly resisted in signing the long promised Association Agreement with the EU. However, when Yanukovych, reputed for his corrupt and authoritarian style of governance, responded to the peaceful protests by violent repression, protestors at Euromaidan demanded the President's resignation.

On January 16, 2014, Yanukovych-led Party of Regions together with the Communists voted for the so-called 'draconian laws,' in a way which violated all the procedures and regulations, as well as the Constitution. These laws sharply restricted independent mass media, civil society activists, think tanks and NGOs. In fact, it legalized large-scale repression against all who were opposed to Yanukovych.

In February 2014, security forces started to shoot protesters. According to the agreement signed between the opposition and President Yanukovych on February 21, 2014, the Parliament returned to the 2004 constitutional reforms and the outcome represented a parliamentary-cum-presidential form of government. This reversal was one of the demands of Euromaidan. Yanukovych (and not the opposition as Kremlin claimed) violated this agreement: he did not sign parliamentary decision and fled to Russia.

It is important to stress that sometimes Euromaidan was viewed as struggle between the West and Russia. However, the West started sanctions only after Yanukovych became responsible for the death of almost one hundred demonstrators in one day in Kyiv. After that he left the country. It can be concluded that events at Euromaidan were the result of internal dynamics.

Early presidential elections for May 2014 were scheduled/ratified by the parliament. However, prospects for a successful resolution of these domestic problems were threatened by external factors: the annexation of Crimea by Russia and the subsequent Russian military infiltration in Donbas (the two eastern regions of the country).

Annexation of Crimea and the war in Donbas

Regional authorities in Crimea and Donetsk recognized the new regime in Kyiv. Russian President Vladimir Putin decided to enforce a plan which was prepared well ahead of events in Ukraine. The Russian guideline "For return of Crimea" certified February 20 as the date of commencement of the process when Yanukovych was still in Kyiv as Ukrainian President. Russian soldiers without insignia invaded Crimea. Putin denied the allegation of encroachment but admitted it in a documentary which appeared on Russian TV a year later.[4] Under Russian armed occupation, the pseudo-referendum was held in violation of all Ukrainian laws and international procedure.

It was clear violation of the 1994 Budapest memorandum: Ukraine gave up its nuclear arsenal (the third largest in the world) in exchange for "security assurances" to its territorial integrity given by the US, the UK, and Russia (France and China issued relevant statements later). The parties agreed to respect Ukraine's borders, to abstain from the use or threat of force against Ukraine, to support Ukraine where an attempt is made to place pressure on it by economic coercion and to bring any incident of aggression by a nuclear power before the UN Security Council.[5]

It also became the first case of an annexation in Europe occurring since the end of World War II.[6] Many commentators compared it to the 1938 *Anschluss* of Austria and Sudetenland or the 1990 occupation of Kuwait. On March 27, 2014, the UN Assembly General resolution on territorial integrity of Ukraine was supported by 100 countries, with only 11 voting against it (that included North Korea, Sudan, Syria, Bolivia, Cuba, Nicaragua, Zimbabwe, Venezuela, and Belarus). India and China among other 58 countries that abstained, and 24 countries were absent).[7]

Moscow has not taken into account the fate of Crimean Tatars, Sunni Muslim minority and the real natives of Crimea, who strongly supported territorial integrity of Ukraine. Crimean Tatars, deported from Crimea by Stalin in 1944, were not allowed to come back until 1990. After Russian annexation, leaders of Crimean Tatars have not been allowed to come to Crimea. Among them was Mustafa Cemilev (Qirimoglu), who spent 15 years in Soviet prisons and then was head of Crimean Tatar *Mejlis* for 25 years.

Putin wanted to repeat Crimean scenario in other Ukrainian southern and eastern regions. Russian infiltration in Donbas started in April 2014.[8] Russian citizens became leaders of mass rallies which were compared to Maidan-like situation. However, there was a principal difference: Maidan was non-violent for two months and was aimed against corrupt dictator, while the Russia-led separatists immediately resorted to violent tactics like seizure of arms, kidnapping, torture and even killing of people.

However, Putin's plans to either control all of Ukraine or to divide it have failed. The poll conducted in April 2014 confirmed that separatism did not have support in the south and east of the country with the exception of Donbas, but even there supporters of separatism were in the minority (see Table 1).

Map 1 clearly shows that it was not a civil war, and by August 2014 pro-Russian fighters were on the verge of collapse. They were saved only by invasion of Russian regular troops. However, even after that the occupied areas of Donbas comprised only 3 percent of Ukrainian territory.

Table 1: Do you support the idea that your region should secede from Ukraine and join Russia?
(April 2014 poll by the Kyiv International Institute of Sociology)[9]

	South-East as a whole	*Dnipropetrovsk region*	*Donetsk region*	*Zaporizhia region*	*Luhansk region*	*Mykolayiv region*	*Odesa region*	*Kharkiv region*	*Kherson region*
Certainly, yes, I do	7.1	3.7	11.9	2.2	13.2	3.5	3.2	9.2	1.0
Rather, yes	8.3	3.2	15.6	4.0	17.1	3.7	4.0	6.9	2.5
Difficult to say for sure, partly yes, partly no	12.5	6.9	17.3	9.9	12.4	6.0	11.9	17.3	11.4
Rather, no	16.0	13.1	17.3	17.5	20.6	6.7	19.3	16.1	11.1
Certainly, no, I don't	53.7	71.0	34.9	64.0	31.3	78.7	59.5	49.5	73.5
Refuse to Answer	2.4	2.0	3.0	2.5	5.5	1.5	2.2	1.0	0.5

Map 1

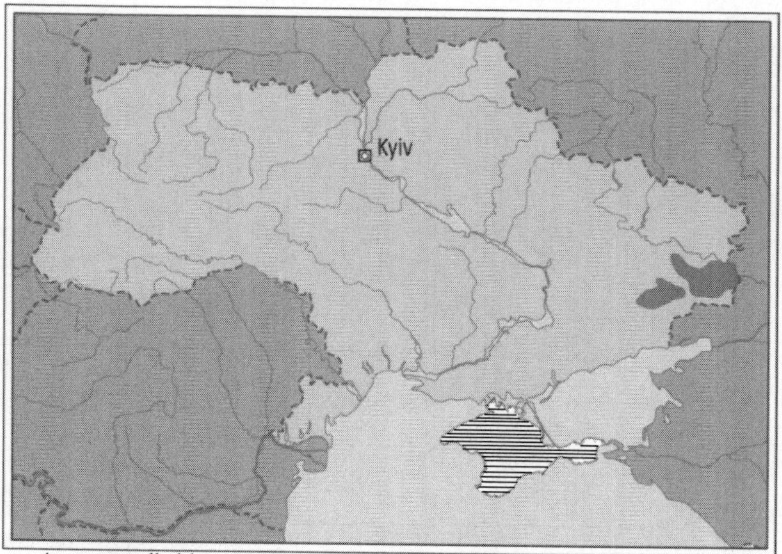

Index: Area controlled by pro-Russian fighters by August 2014 (in dark grey),
The territory of annexed Crimea (in horizontal black stripes)

As the division of Ukraine failed, Moscow decided to impose on Ukraine its 'federalization plan'. However, during the first/initial years of independence it became clear that federalization, attractive as a model for a democratic and multicultural society, could encourage centrifugal tendencies in Ukraine. It is important to note that the 1996 Constitution rejected the idea of federalization. During and after the Orange Revolution the Party of Regions also used the idea of federalization to secure its position in its electoral strongholds to challenge the Orange authorities in Kyiv and also as a campaign slogan (although even the Party of Regions has also decided to avoid mentioning "federalization" in its program). Given the absence of administrative-territorial reform and, therefore, a weak financial basis for self-government, federalization could lead not to development of self-government but to regional parochialism. The key issue for the time being is to strengthen self-government at the local level: village, town, *rayon* (district), but not on *oblast* (region) level. Even in Donbas, the majority favored **decentralization, not federalization** (see table 2).

Table 2: What the state structure of Ukraine should be?

April 2014 poll by the Kyiv International Institute of Sociology[10]

	South-East as a whole	*Dnipropetrovsk region*	*Donetsk region*	*Zaporizhia region*	*Luhansk region*	*Mykolayiv region*	*Odesa region*	*Kharkiv region*	*Kherson region*
Unitary—regions should have the same rights, which they have at the present moment	19.1	19.6	10.6	19.8	12.4	17.9	29.1	23.3	32.9
Unitary, but it is necessary to conduct decentralization of power and broaden rights of regions	45.2	51.0	41.1	51.4	34.2	63.0	44.2	39.1	54.5
Federal	24.8	11.4	38.4	15.3	41.9	10.7	17.5	32.2	6.9
Difficult to say/don't know	8.8	11.6	8.7	13.6	7.9	8.4	8.1	5.2	5.0
Refuse to answer	2.0	6.4	1.2	0.0	3.5	0.0	1.0	0.2	0.7

Ukrainian Political Nation Consolidated

"Reset of power" was a popular slogan of the 'Maidan' movement. Petro Poroshenko, one of prominent 'Maidan' supporters, a businessman and the owner of the opposition TV Channel 5, won a clear cut victory in the first round with 54 percent of the votes. The results of the early presidential elections on May 25, 2014, also proved that the Russian influence has diminished proportionally to Kremlin's involvement in Ukraine. As a result, Poroshenko was the preferred choice in all electoral districts in the eastern and southern Ukraine, except one in the Kharkiv oblast and the separatists'-controlled areas.

The next step was early parliamentary elections. According to the views of the absolute majority of Ukrainians, after unconstitutional laws (see above) these ministers of Parliament had neither the legal nor the moral right to retain their positions. In accordance with Ukrainian Constitution, President Poroshenko announced the date of early parliamentary elections, i.e. October 26, 2014.

However, for the first time in the history of independent Ukraine, elections could not be held on the entire territory of Ukraine. Nevertheless, the empty seats (until it would be possible to organize elections in these areas), only represents a total of 27 out of 450. As 2/3rd of Donbas remained under Ukrainian control, this region received representation on both party slates and single-member constituencies.

One thing was quite predictable: according to all forecasts, pro-European forces won the overwhelming victory, gaining in total almost 70 percent of the vote on party slates. For the first time in independent Ukraine, the Communist Party did not pass the threshold. This party served as the silent "junior partner" of the Party of Regions. Further, the Communist Party was viewed by Ukrainian society as Russia's "fifth column." Moreover, the anti-democratic nature of the Party of Regions and the Communists was only strengthened as soon as information revealed their support for the Russian-backed separatists in Donbas and Crimean annexation.

In general, Ukraine was traditionally a country politically divided between the east and the west. This split was artificially created in the interests of party-politics, as they tried to have control over their own electorate. However, this tendency has started to subside. A more detailed study of regional voting on party slates shows that the south, which traditionally supported Yanukovych, saw the "Maidan" democratic parties beat out the Opposition Bloc and the Communists 2, 5 : 1. Even in the east, the "Maidan" parties were ahead of their opponents. These results testify to the fundamental shifts in the political orientations of Ukrainians after Euromaidan.[11]

The Kremlin uses many kinds of false statements to justify its aggressive stance against Ukraine and annexation of Crimean peninsula. One of which is that Euromaidan was a gathering of far-right extremists. However, Euromaidan events confirmed that modern Ukrainian nationalism is inclusive one and is based not on ethnicity but on territorial identity. In the Maidan, multi-confessional common prayers were held. Ethnic Russians, Jews, other ethnic minorities actively joined the ranks of protesters. Therefore, "the heavy focus on right-wing radicals [in Maidan] in international media reports was misleading."[12]

The paradox is that despite the war in Donbas, Putin's aggression actually cemented political Ukrainian identity, notwithstanding the linguistic or religious origins of Ukrainians. Russian-speakers and locals from Donbas comprise a substantial part of volunteer battalions fighting in Donbas for the territorial integrity of Ukraine. In the parliamentary elections *The Right Sector* secured only 2 percent (just compare to 25 percent of the National Front in France during the elections to the Europarliament). The far right elected only 3 Ministers of Parliament out of a total of 450. The nationalist center-right "Svoboda" (Freedom) also did not overcome/achieve the barrier/the required number of votes.[13] And, despite allegations by the Russian media, no extreme rightist parliamentarian obtained a seat in the cabinet.

At the same time, the new elections produced an overwhelming pro-European majority even if there are still risks of a split in the coalition. The new coalition received 302 seats, which potentially represents a constitutional majority (300 out of 450). Moreover, a broad coalition prevents the monopolization of power by one political party or faction. The challenges are plenty, as the President and the new government need to conduct unpopular reforms in the context of a war-time economy when Russia continues its efforts to destabilize the young Ukrainian democracy.

The new coalition based on the 'coalition agreement' has agreed that European and Euro-Atlantic integration are at the top of Ukraine's foreign policy priorities. These new foreign policy objectives reflect the dramatic shift in Ukrainian society over the past year. Previously, in Ukraine, supporters of NATO membership were always a minority group. However, the non-bloc stance adopted by Yanukovych in 2010 did not prevent Russia's limitless economic and information propaganda against Yanukovych himself in the summer-fall of 2013 when he was about to sign the Association Agreement with the EU. Logically, since the annexation of Crimea, the number of NATO supporters has grown exponentially. According to the November 2014 poll of the "Rating Group," if a referendum was held, it would be 51 percent in favor and 21 percent opposed to joining NATO. Support for EU membership is even higher. In July 2014, 61 percent of Ukrainians would say "yes," while only 20 percent would support joining the Customs Union with Russia.[14]

As the non-bloc status did not prevent from Russian aggression, it has been cancelled by the new parliament in December 2014. At the same time, there is an understanding among Ukrainian politicians and experts that NATO and the EU membership are not on the agenda right now. The emphasis is now on implementing the ratified Association Agreement with the EU.

Conclusion

Contrary to the stereotypes, the contemporary Ukrainian state proclaimed in 1991 is based not so on ethnicity but on the territorial nation-building. This nationalism is an inclusive one. The events of Maidan 2004 and 2013/2014 have shown that the country is moving to more balanced and democratic political system. In February 2014, a hundred of people died under the EU flags in the center of Kyiv to defend democracy and European choice against corrupt and criminal president Yanukovych supported by Russia.

After the revolution, early presidential and parliamentary elections in Ukraine were held. They were recognized by the international community as free and fair. Ukraine-EU Association Agreement which was signed and ratified after the Revolution provides a roadmap for reforms. However, an effective and sustainable Ukrainian democracy represents threat to authoritarian Putin's regime. Hence, his efforts to destabilize Ukraine, especially after annexation of Crimea and Russia's attempts to change territorial borders in the east of Ukraine.

The framework for the necessary first steps to finding a solution is provided by two Minsk Trilateral Agreements, signed in September 2014 and in February 2015 by Ukraine, Russia, and the OSCE. The Agreements outline the ceasefire, the withdrawal of foreign mercenaries, illegal military formations from Ukraine, and the OSCE control over Ukrainian-Russian border. However, the Agreements are yet to be implemented.

Since it has faced military aggression, Ukraine requires the support of the international community. There is hope that other free nations of the world which fought for independence with colonial empires can understand what is Ukraine's fighting against terrorism, armed separatism supported from outside and direct foreign aggression.

ENDNOTES

1. Olexiy Haran ed., *Ukraine in Europe: Questions and Answers*, Kyiv: Stylos, 2009, pp. 15-16.
2. *Ibid.*
3. After the 2006 parliamentary elections, Ukraine was recognized in the ratings of Freedom House as the only 'free country' in the CIS. *Freedom in the World,*

Washington, DC: Freedom House, 2006, www.freedomhouse.org/template.cfm?page=15&year=2006

4. During Euromaidan and after Russian propaganda works in the most cynical way. For example, taking photos from Lybia or Syria and presenting it as evidences of "violence" from Ukrainian side. For more, see www.stopfake.org/en/
5. *Memorandum on Security Assurances in connection with Ukraine's Accession to the Treaty on the NPT*, UN General Assembly document A/49/765, UN Security Council document S/1994/1399, 19 December 1994
6. Andrew Wilson, *Ukraine Crisis. What It Means for the West*, New Haven and London: Yale University Press, 2014, Introduction, pp. vi-vii.
7. *United Nations General Assembly Resolution 68/262 "Territorial integrity of Ukraine"* http://www.un.org/en/ga/search/view_doc.asp?symbol=A/RES/68/262
8. See, for example, Gen. Philip Breedlove, Supreme Allied Commander, Europe, "Who Are the Men Behind the Masks?", Apr. 17, 2014 http://aco.nato.int/saceur2013/blog/who-are-the-men-behind-the-masks.aspx; NATO Releases Imagery: Raises Questions on Russia's Role in Providing Tanks to Ukraine, June 14, 2014 http://aco.nato.int/statement-on-russian-main-battle-tanks.aspx
9. *Zerkalo Nedeli*, 19 April 2014, p. 6.
10. *Zerkalo Nedeli*....
11. Members of the Party of Regions obtained better results in single-mandate districts, as they used traditional schemes to buy votes. This irregular electoral practice further illustrates the need to move towards a proportional electoral system with open party slates. For more see, Olexiy Haran, Maria Zolkina, "A Year after Euromaidan: Pro-European Forces Wins the New Parliament", *Insight Turkey*, 4 (2014), pp. 33-45.
12. See, the public statement "Kyiv's Euromaidan is a Liberationist and Not Extremist Mass Action of Civic Disobedience", prepared by Dr. Andreas Umland, German academic expert on the far right, and signed by forty Ukrainian and Western academic experts. http://blogs.pravda.com.ua/authors/haran/52f0b14c4cc77/. Also see Volodymyr Kulyk, "Ukrainian Nationalism since the Outbreak of Euromaidan", *Ab Imperio*, 3 (2014), pp. 94-122.
13. True, in the 1990s, "Svoboda" started as a far right force but by the elections of 2012, it moderated its position and moved towards the conservative center-right.
14. Olexiy Haran, Maria Zolkina, 'A Year After EuroMaidan....', pp. 44-45.

BIBLIOGRAPHY

Breedlove, Philip. "Who Are the Men Behind the Masks?", Apr. 17, 2014 http://aco.nato.int/saceur2013/blog/who-are-the-men-behind-the-masks.aspx

Freedom in the World (Washington, DC: Freedom House, 2006).

Haran, Olexiy and Zolkina, Maria. "A Year after Euromaidan: Pro-European Forces Wins the New Parliament", *Insight Turkey*, 4 (2014): 33-45.

Haran, Olexiy (ed.), *Ukraine in Europe: Questions and Answers*, Kyiv: Stylos, 2009.

Kulyk, Volodymyr. "Ukrainian Nationalism since the Outbreak of Euromaidan", *Ab Imperio*, 3 (2014) : 94-122.

Memorandum on Security Assurances in connection with Ukraine's Accession to the Treaty on the NPT, UN General Assembly document A/49/765, UN Security Council document S/1994/1399, 19 December 1994.

United Nations General Assembly Resolution 68/262 "Territorial integrity of Ukraine" http://www.un.org/en/ga/search/view_doc.asp?symbol=A/RES/68/262

Wilson, Andrew, *Ukraine Crisis. What It Means for the West*, New Haven and London: Yale University Press, 2014.

4

Russia, Ukraine: The New Cold War

Critique of America's Manifest Destiny

Premen Addy

Ukraine is at the crossroads, its future uncertain, its ethnic fault-lines dangerously exposed to the deepening turbulence in Russian-NATO relations. The country is a house divided, of conflicting identities – Russian in the industrialized East, non-Russian in the rural West – with combustible angles of vision on a fraught past. The country's Western region, the seedbed of uncompromising nationalism, with its fascist and pro-Nazi colourations, is best exemplified by Stepan Bandera's wartime party and kindred groups, who collaborated with the Nazi occupiers in the murder of Jews and Poles. These extremist elements are the ideological forbears of the present *Pravy Sektor* (Right Sector) and *Svoboda* (Freedom party), both in varying degrees anti-Semitic and much given to railing against the "the Jewish-Russian mafia" in Kiev. *Pravy Sektor* is in denial over its anti-Semitism (which it ascribes to Moscow propaganda), but says it is as "nationalist, defending the values of white, Christian Europe," that it holds multiculturalism "responsible for the disappearance of the crucifix and the arrival of girls in burqas in your school," a view with which *Svoboda* is in fervent accord.

However, *Pravy Sektor*, unlike *Svoboda*, is against joining the European Union.

Among *Svoboda's* priorities is the cultural cleansing of Russian influences in the country, which include banning the teaching of Russian in schools (the country has been, and is, bilingual), abolishing Russian street names, depriving Russian-populated Crimea its autonomy, and joining NATO for the acquisition of modern weaponry. Yulia Tymoshenko, the former President of Ukraine, who fell out with her successor Viktor Yanukovych, and was imprisoned for corruption, as the country's foremost political virago, gave vent on camera to anti-Russian fury, advocating the use of nuclear weapons against the Crimea's Russian population. Yet, it was in Kievan Rus that the Russian state was born; both nations are tied by the umbilical cord of the Orthodox faith, culture and history. Nikolai Gogol, among the titans of 19th century Russian literature, was Ukrainian by birth but Russian in his choice of language. Thousands of Ukrainians today work in Russia – as do Georgians – and send back substantial remittances to their families and dependants.

Troubled waters are where meddlesome great powers most like to fish, no one more so than the United States. Ukraine is where the United States and NATO chose to bait Russia; it was to be the post-Cold War denouement to encircle Russia: to break its resolve and capacity to be an effective rival. NATO's eastward expansion violated the solemn assurances of Western leaders to Mikhail Gorbachev, then Soviet leader, that no advantage would be taken if Soviet forces were to withdraw from Eastern and Central Europe and permit unified Germany's membership of NATO. Jack Matlock, then United States ambassador in Moscow, has told how the end of the Cold War was a negotiation with the Soviet Union with no winners and losers in mind. Ambassador Matlock deplored the consequent Western triumphalism and the expansion of NATO, which other hallowed veterans of the American establishment, such as George Kennan and Paul Nitze, warned against as needlessly provocative[1]. But with the alcoholic Boris Yeltsin at the helm, the opportunity for the Clinton Administration was one too good to pass. Matlock deplored NATO's decision to bomb and destroy Yugoslavia, arbitrarily detach Kosovo from Serbia, invade Iraq and attack Libya as dangerous precedents from which there would be the inevitable blowback against what the late Senator J William Fulbright titled the "Arrogance of Power."

Straddling foundations, think-tanks, universities and such revered institutions as the Council of Foreign Relations, the Kennedy School at Harvard, the Woodrow Wilson Center, the Nitze School at John Hopkins, the Naval War College, Georgetown University, the Brookings and Carnegie Foundation, the Departments of State and Defense, not to speak of the National Security Council and CIA, are where American grand strategists gather and move seamlessly to and fro, regardless of party sympathies or affiliations, upholding at all times the sacramental truth of "the indispensable power," its "exceptionalism" and its preordained "Manifest Destiny," as the planet's "Liberal Leviathan" or preferred "benign hegemon," surely as fictional a construct as the Unicorn.[2]

These guardians of the sacred flame cogitate endlessly on the conjugal alignments of Theodore Roosevelt's carrot-and-stick realpolitik with Woodrow Wilson's home spun convenience-store democracy, human rights and much else that was (is) palatable and marketable to domestic opinion and to posterity. Both traditions are woven into a scriptural narrative of affirmation and denial. A galaxy of distinguished American historians, political theorists, writers and commentators, from William Appleman Williams, Noam Chomsky, Chalmers Johnson, Gabriel Kolko, Gar Alperovitz, Senator, J. William Fulbright, iconic columnists, Walter Lippmann and I.F. Stone, novelist, essayist and critic, Gore Vidal, to investigative journalists, James Risen, Seymour Hersh, Gary J. Bass, Oliver Stone and collaborator Peter Kuznick, have produced an impressive counter-factual *kulturkritik*, giving a disenchanted public space to grow.

In the infinite present, America's War on Terror has been neutered to "Contingency Operations" by an Obama Presidential Order, matching the George W Bush edict of "Enhanced Interrogation Techniques," palliatives for torture pure and simple. Humanitarian interventions, whether it be in Iraq or Libya have reduced the intended beneficiaries to howling desolations of lawlessness and sectarian strife, with only death as the merciful liberator. Benjamin Rhodes, Obama's speech writer and now deputy national security advisor, has written: "What we're trying to do is to get America another fifty years as leader." The President, a Nobel Peace laureate, has set his sights on making this the American Century.

Zbigniew Brzezinski, Polish American strategist and former national security advisor in the Carter Administration, having cast on the vast Eurasian landscape, proclaimed that China was key to America's containment of Russia and of India[3], that the defining contest of wills between Washington and Moscow would be Ukraine. It would be no bad thing for Russia to be sliced into three sovereign entities, with eastern Siberia colonized by vibrant West European youth, the majority, preferably, fevered Polish Catholic nationalists.

President Vladimir Putin, clearly, was no mute spectator to the turmoil in Kiev's Maidan, with the European Union and American great and good stoking the embers into an uncontrolled blaze. The putsch that followed in February 2014 sent President Yanakovych fleeing to Russia. A transfixed world waited for the bugle call of triumph. Putin, responded with the speed and decisiveness of a chess grandmaster: Russian special forces entered Crimea, disarmed Ukraine's military bases with the loss of a solitary Ukrainian life, maintained order with help from the local citizenry, turncoat constabulary and military formations, while the Crimean legislature made a swift declaration of independence, followed by an overwhelming vote to join the Russian Federation, both confirmed with equal dispatch by an honest referendum witnessed firsthand by Austrian MEP Ewald Stadler and other observers of repute.

The constitutional process was appropriately sealed in one of the most ornate rooms in the Kremlin; rhapsodic expressions of public joy in Moscow and other Russian cities greeted the historic event. Mikhail Gorbachev, the Cold War peacemaker, told of his delight at the Crimea's return to the Russian family, the 60-year separation – ordained by Nikita Khrushchev in 1954 – at an end. Crimea[4] was where the *Wehrmacht* and the Red Army stretched each other's utmost limits of courage and endurance in a year-long struggle for supremacy, hence the Crimean soil is as sacred to Russian memory as the epic sieges of Moscow and Leningrad and the Homeric battles of Stalingrad and Kursk. Co-habitation with Nazi sympathizers strained credulity.

Ukraine's crisis bears more than a passing likeness to the situation on the Indian Subcontinent in 1971: West Pakistan for Western Ukraine, East Pakistan for Eastern Ukraine; with US President Richard Nixon and his National Security Advisor, Henry Kissinger, resolutely opposed to self-determination for the Bengali East Pakistan, callously indifferent to the slaughter of the local population by the West Pakistan army and its armed thugs, content merely to point the finger of blame at India.

As America's five billion dollar democracy project for Ukraine crumbles, ashes to ashes, dust to dust, the country's future configuration is uncertainly poised. Kiev's intensifying "War on Terror" in Eastern Ukraine, encouraged with unbridled zeal by Obama and his colleagues, portends Ukraine's descent into the abyss. Three centuries ago, Alexander Pope composed these prescient lines: "*Lo! thy dread Empire, Chaos! Is restor'd; / Light dies before the uncreating word; /Thy hand great Anarch! Lets the curtain fall; /And Universal Darkness buries All.*"[5]

Following the dissolution of the Soviet Union, President George H.W. Bush issued this heraldic proclamation, "A world once divided into two armed camps now recognizes one, sole and pre-eminent power, the United States of America."[6] It was the end of history, intoned Francis Fukuyama, samurai chronicler of Uncle Sam's last hurrah before the

American nirvana entombed humankind in its chill embrace. When Alexander Solzhenitsyn returned to his native Russia after long exile in the United States, he was struck by the distress around him. The author of *The Gulag Archipelago* was convinced of America's will to strip and dismember the Russian world. This was not how it seemed when the Berlin Wall came tumbling down in June 1989, and "Gorby mania" held German crowds in thrall. Mikhail Gorbachev, hailed as peacemaker extraordinary, sank into predetermined oblivion when his work was done and dusted. The demolition of Yugoslavia by NATO followed in due course. Marshal Tito, hailed during his lifetime as a hero-liberator in the war against Nazi Germany, alongside the Western Allies, came to be reviled after his death as an evil communist dictator, when plans were afoot to destroy Yugoslavia. Winston Churchill, Britain's pre-eminent wartime prime minister, spoke of Joseph Stalin as a great leader with a saving sense of humour, marked by an absence of illusions; Gorbachev, alas, and Tito before him, in their different ways, succumbed to their respective illusions of Western good faith. Margaret Thatcher, another British prime minister, described Gorbachev as someone with whom the West "can do business." And so it proved. The living Gorbachev has time to rue the past; Tito is condemned to ghostly reflection, while the shade of the mirthful Stalin is possibly having the last laugh.

Vladimir Putin's emergence as President of the Russian Federation in the new millennium opened a chapter of seed time and remedy: the economy was soon in recovery, the international debt default was repaid, national confidence returned. The President's first foreign policy demarche, directed at India, included annual bilateral summits, to be held alternately in Moscow and New Delhi, an elevated vision of the Indo-Russian relationship fit for purpose in the 21st century. Sino-Russian ties, blighted for decades by bitter ideological disputes and political suspicion, were normalized. That was a turnaround of considerable significance for, between 1971 and 2000, China and the United States had been de facto allies, wedded to the containment of the Soviet Union, and to India's confinement within the circumscribed limits of the Subcontinent. In contrast, India has enjoyed a trouble-free relationship, spanning 67 years, with every regime in Moscow. Prime Minister Narendra Modi stated recently, that India and Russia were bonded by a "friendship of unmatched mutual confidence, trust and goodwill," and that their "strategic partnership is incomparable in content." Moscow's leading role in the formation of BRICS and the Shanghai Cooperation Organization signalled Russia's pivot to Asia, where new vistas in trilateral engagement between Russia, India and China point to untapped possibilities for the construction of an equitable, multi-polar world order.

However, President Putin also made approaches to the United States and its NATO allies, permitting the use of Russian territory as a strategic transit for their forces in Afghanistan waging war against the jihadi Taliban. Putin's overtures to the United States for a post-Cold War alignment based on partnership and trust were spurned. At the heart of the junior Bush administration were gung-ho neo-conservative hawks, among them Paul Wolfowitz, Dick Cheney and Donald Rumsfeld. As assistant secretary of defence in the senior Bush administration (1988-92), Wolfowitz had cut his teeth as a strategic thinker with a controversial policy paper stating that the United States would accept no future rival to its global dominance, that pre-emption might follow if one were to appear. Wolfowitz, Cheney and Rumsfeld were the movers and shakers in Washington as the United States embarked on its wars of intervention in Iraq and Afghanistan; these and the Obama administration's forays in Libya and Syria and now, Yemen, have contributed exponentially to the present rise of the Islamic State Caliphate or ISIL. Moscow's rapier thrust in Crimea, subsequent to the Western-supervised *coup de main* in Kiev, carried a robust message, which led *Le Monde diplomatique* to editorialize[7] that the era of America's diktat "is now over. Its death knell sounded the day Russia had enough of 'losing' and realized that its ritual humiliation would never come to an end, with one neighbouring country after another being persuaded – or bribed – into joining an economic and military alliance against it."

Speaking in Brussels in March 2014, President Obama stressed that, "Today, NATO planes patrol the skies over the Baltic and we've reinforced our presence in Poland. And we are prepared to do more." The Cold War mutant is now the media's "New Cold War," with its altered focus for, says Obama, "unlike the Soviet Union, Russia leads no bloc of nations, no global ideology." The admission carried a deeper truth: Russia, being Russia, is a massively enduring obstacle to the global hegemony of any power. For Adolf Hitler, compromise with a reduced France or Britain was conceivable, but *untermenschen* Russia, which merited no such consideration, had to be removed forthwith as living space for the master race. For Russia there could be nothing but absolute war and total extermination. "The offence of Russia was theexistence of Russia," wrote the English historian Hugh Trevor Roper.[8] The Soviets rose, phoenix-like, from the ruins of the Nazi assault to become the colossus reborn, bent on punishing the Nazi violator of the Motherland.

Obama appears to hymn Kipling's Great Game, minus the 19th century romance, yet, beneath its velvet glove of pietas exists, surely, the cloven hoof of 21st century aggrandisement. In November 2010, US Admiral James G. Stavridis spoke of a possible conflict with Russia over control of the Arctic's immense resources of oil, gas and rare earths. The policy platform was the Presidential Directive by George W. Bush, in January 2009, calling for the "deployment of sea and air systems for strategic airlift, strategic deterrence, maritime presence, and maritime security (to) preserve the global mobility of the United States military and civilian vessels and aircraft throughout the Arctic region," including the North Sea route along Russia's Arctic coast, which Moscow regards as a national waterway. The battle has been well and truly joined, with Russia restoring and modernizing its defunct post-Cold War northern bases: Borei submarines and Bulava-class long range missiles are their sentinels. Already, Russian super-tankers and commercial vessels traverse the Arctic waters from Europe to Asia, 9,000 km less than the traditional route through the Suez Canal. By 2020, projects an official document in Moscow, the polar expanse will become Russia's "main strategic resource base."

The more things change, the more they remain the same, is a timeless Gallic aphorism. Niall Ferguson, the Harvard-based British historian has argued in his work, *Colossus: The Rise and Fall of the American Empire*, that America would be better served dispensing with its pharisaic overload of morality, accepting, indeed welcoming, the responsibilities of its *imperium*. Witness the Monroe doctrine of 1823, the warning to European powers against intruding into America's hallowed space, setting in train decades of American westward expansion to the Pacific Ocean, much of the territory acquired through outright conquest, blandishment and the voluntary accession of white settlements. Ethnic cleansing of indigenous peoples, and the confinement of their indigent descendants to arid reservations, were concomitants to the commerce in black slavery and the sequential politics of segregation, upheld and sanctified by the courts as statutory law for almost a century after the end of the American civil war (1861-65). Such injustices were applied with the utmost rigour in the southern states, these to be compounded in mid-20th century by Senator Joseph McCarthy's inquisition: each phase a fitting entry in the ledger of corporate America's Manifest Destiny. The rubric of empire is the imprimatur of America's worldly advance, says Ferguson. An extrapolated passage written in 1935 by General Smedley D. Butler, the most decorated American marine commander of his generation, illuminates Ferguson's point.

"I helped make Haiti and Cuba a decent place for the National City Bank boys to collect revenues in. I helped in the raping of half a dozen Central American republics for the benefit of Wall Street....I helped purify Nicaragua for the international house of Brown Brothers in 1909-1912. I brought light to the Dominican Republic for American sugar interests in 1916. I helped make Honduras 'right' for American companies in 1903....Looking back on it, I feel I might have given Al

Capone a few hints. The best he could do was to operate his racket in three districts. We Marines operated on three continents."[9]

Why resist the unpalatable truth for embellished fiction and risk the internalized trauma that comes with denial, argues Ferguson. An American empire (with an Anglophone construct of Canada, Britain, Australia and New Zealand in tow) was best suited to administer to the needs of benighted humanity. Post-war Germany and Japan, South Korea and Taiwan, are cited beneficiaries of American democratic tutelage and protection; the failed states of, say, Africa had even more to gain from benign American governance and financial aid. From the theatre of the absurd came the soothing televised voice of George W. Bush to the people of Iraq on 10 April 2004: "We will help you build a peaceful and representative government that protects the rights of all citizens.... Iraq will go forward as a unified, independent and sovereign nation."[10] Republican party faithful were assured, in a Presidential speech on 5 November 2005, that: "The establishment of a free Iraq in the heart of the Middle East will be a watershed event in the global democratic revolution...."

The torture chambers of Abu Gharaib and Guantanamo Bay, and the Extraordinary Rendition carried out in the secret dungeons of the Baltic States, Poland and Romania, have a Kafkaesque ambience of sinister purpose, in denial and horror. America's "War on Terror" has trapped the country in a moral maze, writes Pulitzer Prize-winning reporter James Risen. "America has become accustomed to a permanent state of war....while a permanent national security elite rotates among senior government posts, contracting companies, think tanks, and television commentary, opportunities that would disappear if America was suddenly at peace. To most of America, war has become not only tolerable but profitable, and so there is no longer any great incentive to end it."[11]

The march of folly moves on regardless. Thousands of men, women and children have perished, been maimed or rendered homeless in the enveloping inferno of the Greater Middle East. Iraq, Syria, Libya, Yemen, Afghanistan are living through the nightmare of loss and desolation with no end to the dark night. Leon Panetta, a former CIA director and former defence secretary in the Obama Administration likened the tragedy to the Thirty Years War in Germany, in the first half the 17th century. But the conflict there involved nations with an approximate weight of power, each to the other, which in the end tired them out and led to the Peace of Westphalia in 1648, opening the doors to the European Enlightenment. The overwhelming might of the United States and its European allies and the paucity of material wealth and sophistication of their Third World adversaries and clients make the present struggle highly unequalat every level. That said, asymmetrical warfare can also test the resilience of the strong and eventually wear them out. Vietnam remains the primary example of the victim of imperialist aggression transmogrified into the triumphant victor. While it may be eons of time before a heroic saga of such historical proportions is repeated, the withdrawals of the US-led military coalitions from Afghanistan and Iraq were surely caused by exhaustion and declining morale, not to speak of the drain on the hard pressed exchequer. Austerity-crippled Greece, Italy, Spain, Portugal and a restive France, has deepened popular disillusionment with the existing trans-Atlantic order. The Western powers will have to endure the karmic fallout from those they have despoiled and ruined.

Libya was subjected to merciless aerial bombardment by NATO squadrons to make the country's huge oil revenues fit for the cynical purposes of the West. Now a wasteland of competing jihadi tribes, clans and factions, some home-grown, others, like ISIL - which recently beheaded a line of Coptic Christian Ethiopians – Libya has become the beachhead, from where thousands of dispossessed migrants from North and Sub-Saharan Africa and regions beyond, embark on their perilous voyage across the deep to the shores of southern Europe: staging posts for onward migration to the hallucinatory El Dorado of the continent's colder north. Tens and hundreds of hapless humanity –

victims of traffickers and their own black despair – have been swallowed by the Mediterranean swell, their unseaworthy vessels – little more than fragile coffins – yielding to the forces of nature. What price freedom and liberal values, what price the gulf between the moralizing bromides of the *Herrenvolk* great and good, and the bleak, unwelcoming reality that awaits the surviving boat people?

This is all of a piece with the Ukraine experience which refracts an epochal struggle for a unipolar world dominated by the United States and its European and kindred satraps elsewhere. The Minsk peace accords have been received with ill-concealed disdain by the Obama Administration and the American political class. The country's military industrial complex searches avidly for new worlds to subdue, so that armament stocks can be replenished with new and deadlier weaponry. The US Administration undermined the first Minsk accord of September 2014 by cynically arming and encouraging Kiev to restart the conquest of its lost territories to the East, a misadventure that cost the regime dear. No lessons learned, an elite US task-force arrived in Ukraine in February 2015 to train and help the local National Guard undermine the second Minsk agreement. The American visitors were given a rapturous welcome by Ukrainian President Petro Porashenko, always a sucker for redemptive salvation from afar. Not surprisingly, Ukraine's shambolic regime has put the Ukranian economy into precipitous free fall: bankrupt, debt-ridden, inflation-prone and going nowhere. It brings to mind the possible appearance of a fifth horseman of the Apocalypse riding to a fateful tryst with the celebrated Four, and Armageddon. Who will step up and keep refinancing Kiev's mounting debt? Not the World Bank, not the International Monetary Fund or the reluctant German bankers, for sure. Should the present US military intervention in the region reignite the civil war in Eastern Ukraine, Chancellor Angela Merkel, who put in so much work and political capital into Minsk diplomacy, will surely feel belittled. So, too, will French President Francoise Hollande, the other major European investor in Minsk II. A durable European peace is being steam rollered by the bullying American behemoth. The French thinker Emmanuel Todd writes: "Let the present America expend what remains of its energy, if that is what it wants to do, 'war on terrorism' – a substitute battle for the perpetuation of hegemony that it has already lost. If it stubbornly decides to continue showing off its supremacy, it will end up exposing to the world its powerlessness."[12] But that is to anticipate history, always fraught with risk for the historian, although not for the star-gazer.

Todd likened the United States to a listing hulk weighed down by its imperial burdens[13]. Reams of print on the imminent demise of the long "dying bear," possibly emboldened Washington to pressgang European Union heads into the delusional sanctions regime against Russia, which US Vice President Joseph Biden, boasted to his youthful Harvard University audience, was an exemplary demonstration of American leadership. Such intimidation is unlikely to work now anymore than it did when President Harry Truman approved the dropping of an atom bomb on the Japanese cities of Hiroshima and Nagasaki in August 1945, on the assumption that an economically devastated Soviet Union, awed by their destructive power, would capitulate to Washington's diktat on the post-war European order. This was the curtain raiser to the Cold War and the arms race, each a progenitor of the spectre of nuclear annihilation. The obscenity of the American nuclear assault, the first and only instance of its kind so far to have disfigured planet earth, was a crime against Japanese humanity, and a traumatic awakening for those who cherish life and its sanctities.[14]

A century and more earlier, the French Emperor Napoleon Bonaparte, believing his Continental System – the commercial blockade of Britain – to be rendered ineffective by Tsarist Russia's non-compliance, embarked on an inebriating invasion of the country to enforce compliance in June 1812: the hubristic exercise ended in the rout of the vaunted Grand Army from the heart of Moscow all the way to Paris, and the nemesis of Waterloo. Fast forward, Adolf Hitler's satanic design to reduce the Soviet Union to an enslaved Slavic desolation of hewers of wood and drawers of water ended in the *Gotterdammerung* of Berlin, May 1945. The fantastical 1,000-year Third Reich closed to the unrelenting timeline of 3 years, 9 months, and 17 days. The imposing force projection capability demonstrated at the military parade in Moscow on 9 May 2015, in celebration of the 70th anniversary of Soviet Union's, Russian-led victory in the Great Patriotic War, and the display of contemporary Russia's military might in Syria, epitomize its resolve to counter any possible delusional repeat by NATO of the *Wehrmacht's* ill-conceived *Operation Barbarossa*, of June 1941. The Russian bear is best not baited.

ENDNOTES

1. Jack Matlock, *Washington Post*, February 27, 2014.
2. Perry Anderson *American Foreign Policy And Its Thinkers*, *New Left Review*, London September/October 2013.
3. Zbigniew Brzezinski, *The Grand Chessboard: American Primacy And Its Geostrategic Imperatives*, New York: Basic Books, 1997, p. 187.
4. Marshal Sergei Biryuzov, 'The Liberation of Crimea' in Prof. John Erickson ed *Main Front: Soviet Leaders Look Back on World War II,* University of Edinburgh, London: Brassey's Defence Publishers, 1987.
5. *The Dunciad* Book IV.
6. *Le Monde Diplomatique*, September 2014.
7. Le Monde Diplomatique....
8. Hugh Trevor-Roper, *The Last Days Of Hitler*, London: Macmillan, 1987, p. 57.
9. Niall Ferguson, *Colossus: The Rise And Fall Of The American Empire*, New York: Penguin Books, 2005, p. 7.
10. Ferguson, *Colossus*.....p. 200.
11 James Risen, *Pay Any Price: Greed, Power, And Endless War*, Boston, New York: Houghton Mifflin Harcourt, 2014, p. xv.
12. Emmanuel Todd, *After The Empire: The Breakdown of the American Order*, p. 202.
13. Todd, pp. 198-199.
14. Alexander Werth, *Russia at War*, pp. 1044-45; see also Gar Alperovitz, *The Decision to Use the Atom Bomb and the Architecture of an American Myth,* London: Harper Collins, 1995, pp. 3-5.

BIBLIOGRAPHY

Alperovitz, Gar. *The Decision To Use the Atomic Bomb and the Architecture of an American Myth*, London: HarperCollins, 1995

Bass, Gary J. *The Blood Telegram: Nixon, Kissinger And A Forgotten Genocide*, New York: Alfred A. Knopf, 2014

Biryuzov, Marshal Sergei. 'The Liberation of Crimea' in Prof. John Erickson ed *Main Front: Soviet Leaders Look Back on World War II*, University of Edinburgh, London: Brassey's Defence Publishers, 1987

Bellamy, Chris. *Absolute War: Soviet Russia in the Second World War*, London: Pan Books, 2007

Brzezinski, Zbigniew. *The Grand Chessboard: American Primacy And Its Geostrategic Imperatives*, New York: Basic Books, 1997

Chomsky, Noam. *American Power and the New Mandarins*, London: Pelican Books, 1969

Coll, Steve. *Ghost Wars*, New York: The Penguin Press, 2004

Cooley, John K. *Unholy Wars: Afghanistan, America and International Terrorism*, London: Pluto Press, 1999

Ferguson, Niall. *Colossus: The Rise and Fall Of The American Empire*, New York: Penguin Books, 2005

Fulbright, J. William. *The Arrogance of Power*, London: A Pelican Book, 1970

Hosking, Geoffrey. *Russia and The Russians: From Earliest Times To 2001*, London: Penguin Books, 2001

Johnson, Chalmers. *Blowback: The Costs and Consequences of American Empire*, Henry Holt and Company, Canada: Owl Book edition, 2001

Kleveman, Lutz. *The New Great Game*, New York: Atlantic Monthly Press, 2003

Risen, James. *Pay Any Price: Greed, Power, And Endless War*, Boston, New York: Houghton Mifflin Harcourt, 2014

Trevor Roper, Hugh. *The Last Days of Hitler*, London: Macmillan, 1987

Sood, Vikram and Kurginyan, Sergey eds., *Radical Islam: Perspectives from India and Russia*, New Delhi: Observer Research Foundation, 2011

Stone, Olivier and Kuznick, Peter. *The Untold History of The United States*, USA: Ebury Press, 2012

Todd, Emmanuel. *After The Empire: The Breakdown of The American Order*, New York: Columbia University Press, 2002

Werth, Alexander. *Russia At War 1941-1945*, New York: Carroll & Graff Publishers, 1964

Williams, William Appleman. *The Tragedy of American Diplomacy*, New York: W.W. Norton & Company, 1959

5

Crisis in Ukraine: A Russian Perspective

Ajay Kamalakaran

Introduction

The tragic events of the last 14 months in the former Soviet republic of Ukraine have already claimed 6,000[1] lives, and displaced more than a million people.

The US-backed Western media has largely and widely reported that Russia is arming, aiding and even commanding the rebels in Eastern Ukraine.

Going by such media reports and the official Ukrainian narrative, a casual observer would be inclined to think that Russia is both the initiator and the principal aggressor in the conflict.

This paper aims to look at the underlying cause of the conflict in Ukraine and the way it has shaped up over the last year, but with a Russian perspective, so as to present the other side of the story. It is also the aim of this writer to suggest a workable solution, implementable by all sides, which could bring long-lasting peace in the country.

NATO Expansion and the 2014 Coup in Ukraine

Russian experts will be quick to argue that one of the root causes of the current crisis in Ukraine is the enlargement of the North Atlantic Treaty Organization (NATO).

In his article[2], Russian foreign policy expert Alexander Lukin writes that in the months following the collapse of the Berlin Wall, the United States formally promised the Soviet Union that the alliance would not expand eastwards if once the USSR withdrew troops from East Germany.

Both American analysts and government officials have denied such a claim. However it goes without say that at a time when Russia was at its weakest, the trans-Atlantic alliance moved eastwards absorbing one former Warsaw Pact member after another. Since 1990, NATO has added 10 countries, including Poland, the Czech Republic and the former Baltic members of the Soviet Union.

Effectively NATO has entered the gates of Russia and is looking to add Finland, Moldova, Sweden and Georgia. It's hardly surprising that Russia considers this enlargement a serious threat and an attempt at encirclement.

In a scathing attack on America's (and NATO's) foreign policy, renowned New York Times journalist Thomas Friedman wrote[3]: "I opposed expanding NATO toward Russia after the Cold War, when Russia was at its most democratic and least threatening. It remains one of the dumbest things we've ever done and, of course, laid the groundwork for Putin's rise."

Russian President Vladimir Putin watched the expansion of NATO with growing alarm and has always been vocal against this enlargement, which he logically sees as nothing but an attempt to encircle or entrap Russia. Yet the expansion eastwards of the trans-Atlantic alliance did not directly threaten Russia until the events of February 2014 that led to a coup in Ukraine.

The coup led to the ouster of the democratically elected Viktor Yanukovych government in Ukraine and the insertion of a regime that would push for the country to become a member of NATO.

The US Assistant Secretary of State for European and Eurasian Affairs, Victoria Nuland openly admitted[4] at the US-Ukraine Foundation Conference in December 2013 that America was sponsoring the events in the Maidan in Kyiv that would eventually lead to a coup.

"Since Ukraine's independence in 1991, the United States has supported Ukrainians as they build democratic skills and institutions, as they promote civic participation and good governance, all of which are preconditions for Ukraine to achieve its European aspirations," Nuland said at the conference. "We've invested over $5 billion to assist Ukraine in these and other goals that will ensure a secure and prosperous and democratic Ukraine." Nuland has made similar statements during television interviews.

It was abundantly clear that the ultimate aim of America to add Ukraine to the Trans-Atlantic alliance was to evict the Russian Black Sea Fleet from its bases in the Crimean Peninsula, where the Russian Navy had a presence for over 230 years.

A NATO base in Sevastopol would have effectively led to cutting off Russia from warm water access to the Mediterranean Sea and onwards to the Atlantic Ocean.

Given the urgency that the newly installed government in Kiev showed in asserting their right to join NATO, Russia was left with few options to protect its geopolitical and strategic interests.

A year after its swift operation to control Crimea that was a precursor to a referendum in the peninsula, Russian President Vladimir Putin spoke in length about the whole operation in a government-sanctioned documentary. The president claimed that although Crimea was a national security issue for Russia, if the referendum on the peninsula indicated that its residents did not want to return to Russia, that the territory would not have been taken back.

Putin admitted that the plans were hatched as soon as it became clear that Ukrainian President Viktor Yanukovych was likely to buckle under pressure from the protestors in Kiev who wanted to a regime change.

Although just a handful of countries recognized the accession of Crimea into Russia, powerful countries such as China and India refused to both condemn the "annexation" and be a part of the sanctions that were imposed on Russia by Western countries.

It must be noted that the return of Crimea to Russia was a well-executed plan that resulted in no deaths. What broke the back of the Ukrainian government's resistance was the fact that there was large popular sentiment in Crimea for a return to Russia, in addition to several defections of top Ukrainian armed forces personnel, including the country's own naval chief.

It was also obvious that the US and NATO were not going to risk a nuclear war with Russia to recapture the peninsula, which was only a part of Ukraine from 1954, when the Supreme Soviet under Nikita Khrushchev transferred the peninsula to the then Ukrainian Soviet Socialist Republic.

American analysts even suggested that the Crimean annexation by Russia, as they put it, be considered a fait accompli.

War in Eastern Ukraine

One of the main reasons that there was a growing anxiety in Crimea after the February Kiev 2014 coup was the actual mobilization of far right parties in Ukraine. It was widely believed by Russian speakers in Ukraine that the street protests that led to the overthrow of Viktor Yanukovych were largely mobilized by the Ukrainian party *Svoboda* (Freedom) and *Pravyi Sektor* (Right Sector), a group that follows Nazi ideology.

These connections between the Ukrainian right with neo-Nazi ideology were highlighted over the first few months of 2014 on Russian state-run television, which has a wide following both in Crimea as well as the eastern regions of Ukraine, which border Russia.

Irresponsible statements by the post-coup leaders on the curtailed usage of the Russian language no doubt fanned fears in Crimea as well as border regions in eastern Ukraine. The protestors' use of strong anti-Russian rhetoric during the coup in Kiev further created insecurities.

Around the time fresh elections were announced in Ukraine, protestors that the West claimed were backed by Russia began to occupy public buildings in the Donbass region cities of Lugansk and Donetsk. These protests were largely seen as peaceful, although there were sporadic incidents of violence.

Initial Ukrainian troops sent to these cities were met with public resistance and initial reports showed the troops defecting to the side of the protestors. As the presidential election grew closer, the protestors in eastern Ukraine, who the West claimed were supported by Russia, intensified their seizure of public buildings and protests against the Kiev authorities. Sporadic incidents of violence then began to break out with both sides trading blame.

Odessa Killings and Petro Poroshenko's Presidency

The unrest in eastern Ukraine spread from the Russian border regions to the Ukrainian Black Sea city of Odessa. On May 2, 2014, riots between pro-Russian protestors and their pro-Ukrainian counterparts led to the deaths of 48 people.

42 unarmed pro-Russia activists were burned to death[5] in the city's Trade Union's House when Molotov's cocktails were hurled at the buildings by pro-Ukrainian activists.

Russian Television station RT[6] interviewed survivors of the massacre, who said radicals set the building with people inside on fire in Odessa, then strangled the survivors and finished them with bats, while police did nothing to prevent the bloodshed.

Witnesses told the station that pro-autonomy activists wanted to hide from the pro-Ukraine protestors by barricading themselves in the building. The report added that the number of pro-government supporters increased and some of them began hurling Molotov cocktails, after which the first and the third floors of the House of Trade Unions burst into flames.

Tatyana also recalled that the outraged crowd outside was shouting that they wouldn't let anybody out.

"The police were idle not doing anything," Tatyana Ivananko, a survivor of the incident told RT. "When firefighters arrived it was too late – too many people had already died, even though the closest fire station is 700 meters away from the site."

In 11 months since what was called the Odessa Massacre, the Ukrainian authorities are yet to prosecute a single person. Many analysts argue that the massacre created a permanent scar in Ukrainian society between ethnic Ukrainians and Russian speakers.

Petro Poroshenko, the man who would win Ukraine's presidential elections later that month, blamed local and Russian officials for the violent events that unfolded in Odessa that day. It was an ominous sign that the soon to be president would adopt a hardline against rebels in the south and east of Ukraine.

Poroshenko, an oligarch and chocolate baron, was elected as president on a pro-Europe and anti-Russia platform. He insisted that Ukraine would not give up the Crimean peninsula and also said the country would move forward with an association agreement with the European Union. It was Yanukovych's dilly-dallying on the agreement that led to protests in Kiev, which culminated in the 2014 coup.

It was widely believed in the restive Ukrainian regions that Poroshenko had the backing of Ukraine's ultra right wing and neo-

Nazi groups and political parties. It must be noted that the Svoboda party did not have much success in the subsequent parliamentary elections held in Ukraine later in the year, falling 0.3 percent short of the minimum 5 percent of votes to enter the parliament. The Right Sector, which formed its own political party made gains and won 1.8 percent.

Noted Ukrainian sociologist Volodymyr Ishchenko wrote in the Guardian[7] that while the Russian terming of the ruling establishment in Ukraine as the Kiev junta was nothing short of propaganda, "the indifference of officials and mainstream opinion to the election of far-right MPs is hugely worrying."

Ishchenko added, "It is short-sighted and formalistic to conclude that the Ukrainian far right is insignificant based on the lack of electoral success. The rhetoric of many politicians, which could be called centrist or even liberal has moved significantly to the right, competing for the increasingly patriotic and even nationalist voters. There were a number of incidents of hate speech used even by top Ukrainian politicians ..."

Within days of Poroshenko's inauguration, hostilities commenced between the rebels in eastern Ukraine and the Ukrainian Army. It is very unlikely that the president would have called for an all out assault on the rebels without the backing of the US. The resistance of the rebels, though, would have initially stumped those in America directing the Ukrainian government.

The rebels were only using arms that were seized and stolen from the army, but the sheer way they were organized and the resistance they put up, had both Ukraine and its American backers insisted that Russia was directly involved in the conflict.

Several rounds of sanctions were introduced on Russia by the US and some European nations, as a result of the fighting. The fighting, which only recently, came to a halt after a second round of peace talks were held in the Belarusian capital of Minsk, has claimed more than 6000, mostly civilians.

While no irrefutable proof has been provided of Russia's direct role in arming and training Ukrainian separatists, there have been admissions from the rebels that volunteers from the Russian army have been fighting on their side.

Aleksandr Zakharchenko, Chairman of the Council of Ministers of the self-proclaimed Donetsk People's Republic told[8] RT that 3-4000 Russian volunteers were fighting with the rebels. "They [Russian volunteers] are among us, people of Donbass because we are blood brothers," Zakharchenko said. "There is no secret that among the volunteers from Russia there are many military men. They are fighting together with us because they understand that it's their duty.

The BBC reported[9] that French, Spanish, Swedish and Serbian volunteers are fighting for both sides in the conflict.

Mikael Skillt, a Swedish sniper with far-right views told the BBC that he was fighting for the Ukrainian government because he believed in the "survival of white people." He added, "I would be an idiot if I said I did not want to see survival of white people… After World War Two, the victors wrote their history. They decided that it's always a bad thing to say I am white and I am proud."

The official American position is that it is not supplying arms to Ukraine, but similar denials were made even in the case of Syrian rebels, many of which have used American weapons to form the Islamic State. American officials told *The New York Times*[10] that there was growing consensus among the US establishment to provide lethal assistance to the Ukrainian army.

In addition to military assistance, the US launched what it termed as Operation Fearless Guardian.[11] Under this six-month operation, 290 paratroopers from the US army's 173rd Airborne Brigade plan to hold joint exercises with 900 Ukrainian soldiers.

"This is the first Ukrainian-American programme at this level, and it shows the transition of bilateral military cooperation into a fundamentally new dimension," Ukrainian President Petro Poroshenko said on Twitter.[12]

Disputed Allegations and Blame Game

MH 17 Shooting

Few incidents brought the crisis in Ukraine to the global spotlight as much as the shooting down of Malaysia Airlines flight MH 17, which was on its way from Amsterdam to Kuala Lumpur on July 17, 2014. The Boeing 777-200 ER airliner was shot in Ukrainian airspace and claimed the lives of 283 passengers and 15 crew members.

While there have been accusations and counter-accusations, the final results of an investigation being conducted by the Dutch Ministry of Justice will only be known in 2016.

The Ukrainian authorities and the US Secretary of State John Kerry were quick to blame[13] the rebels for shooting down the aircraft. Kerry said US intelligence reports provided evidence that Russia provided the rebels with the sophisticated anti-aircraft systems used to down the plane. These claims came within 3 days of the shooting down of the airliner but neutral experts agree that no irrefutable evidence has been presented by either Ukraine or the US.

Within a week of the crash, both America and the European Union imposed a fresh set of sanctions[14] on Russia, blaming the country for providing the rebels with anti-aircraft systems.

It should be noted that Malaysia, which lost 43 citizens and the airliner itself, did not impose sanctions on Russia or blame the country. Statements in Kuala Lumpur indicated a desire to cooperate with both Russia and Ukraine to find out what happened.

Interestingly enough, Malaysia was left out of the Joint Investigation Team (JIT), which was formed under a secret internal agreement between Australia, Holland, Ukraine and even Belgium. Malaysia was only allowed to join the team in December 2014.[15]

While it would be premature to link conspiracy theories to the attack but the fact that Malaysia was not toeing the official Western line may have been responsible for the country's exclusion. Although Malaysia has not blamed either side for the shooting, a report[16] in the New Straits Times cited American intelligence experts as suggesting that the flight was shot down by an air to air missile and that the Ukrainian government had something to do with it.

Given the fact that the media is tightly controlled in Malaysia, a report of such significance would not have been allowed to see the light of day without the consent of the authorities in the country.

The shooting down of the plane brought the civil war in Ukraine to the radar of ordinary citizens around the world and was used as justification for attempts to isolate Russia globally.

Use of Cluster Bombs

In a report published in October 2014, Human Rights Watch[17] said the Ukrainian government forces used cluster munitions in heavily populated areas in the Donetsk region.

"During a week-long investigation in eastern Ukraine, Human Rights Watch documented widespread use of cluster munitions in fighting between government forces and pro-Russian rebels in more than a dozen urban and rural locations," the organization said in the report. "While it was not possible to conclusively determine responsibility for many of the attacks, the evidence points to Ukrainian government forces' responsibility for several cluster munition attacks on Donetsk. An employee of the International Committee of the Red Cross (ICRC) was killed on October 2 in an attack on Donetsk that included use of cluster munition rockets."

Neither the US nor Ukraine count among the 83 countries that have ratified the Convention on Cluster Munitions that calls for a ban on the use of such munitions.

While the toll in the fighting in Ukraine has crossed 6,000, it is clearly difficult to pin point the exact numbers that were killed by either sides, but there is overwhelming evidence like that presented in the Human Rights Watch report that civilian areas have been targeted by the Ukrainian government. Under laws of many countries, the acts committed by the Kiev authorities would comprise of war crimes.

Minsk Accords

Several attempts were made to stop the fighting in Ukraine, including talks between Russian Foreign Minister Sergey Lavrov and US Secretary of State John Kerry. The first meaningful attempt to bring about an end to hostilities in the country was the Minsk Protocol of September 2014.

After extensive talks in the Belarusian capital under the auspices of the Organisation for Cooperation and Security in Europe (OCSE), the Minsk Protocol was signed between representatives of Ukraine, Russia, and the two self-proclaimed republics of Donetsk and Lugansk.

The 12-point protocol was signed by Leonid Kuchma Former president of Ukraine and Ukrainian representative, Mkhail Zubarov, Russian Ambassador to Ukraine and Russian representative, Heidi Tagliavini, Swiss diplomat and OSCE representative and Alexander Zakharchenko and Igor Plotnitsky, the leaders of the Donetsk and Lugansk breakaway republics.

The following 12-points formed the protocol:[18]

1. To ensure an immediate bilateral ceasefire.
2. To ensure the monitoring and verification of the ceasefire by the OCSE.
3. Decentralisation of power, including through the adoption of the Ukrainian law "On temporary Order of Local Self-Governance in Particular Districts of Donetsk and Luhansk Oblasts."

4. To ensure the permanent monitoring of the Ukrainian-Russian border and verification by the OSCE with the creation of security zones in the border regions of Ukraine and the Russian Federation.
5. Immediate release of all hostages and illegally detained persons.
6. A law preventing the prosecution and punishment of persons in connection with the events that have taken place in some areas of Donetsk and Luhansk Oblasts.
7. To continue the inclusive national dialogue.
8. To take measures to improve the humanitarian situation in Donbass.
9. To ensure early local elections in accordance with the Ukrainian law "On temporary Order of Local Self-Governance in Particular Districts of Donetsk and Luhansk Oblasts."
10. To withdraw illegal armed groups and military equipment as well as fighters and mercenaries from Ukraine.
11. To adopt a program of economic recovery and reconstruction for the Donbass region.
12. To provide personal security for participants in the consultations.

Most of these initiatives were blocked mainly because a ceasefire could not be fully implemented, with both sides exchanging blame for the escalation of hostilities.

After intensified fighting in January and February of 2015, the leaders of France, Germany, Russia and Ukraine agreed to measures to halt the on-going civil war. The aim of the new measures was to revive the protocol that was signed in September 2014.

Out of a total of 13 measures[19] adopted as per Minsk II, the following are the highlights:

1. Ceasefire that began at 00:01 local time on February 15.
2. Heavy weapons withdrawal beginning on February 16 and completed in two weeks.

3. Release of all prisoners and amnesty for those involved in fighting.
4. Withdrawal of all foreign troops and weapons from Ukrainian territory, and disarmament of all illegal groups.
5. Ukraine to allow resumption of normal life in rebel areas, by lifting restrictions.
6. Constitutional reform to enable decentralisation for rebel regions by the end of 2015.
7. Ukraine to control border with Russia if conditions met by the end of 2015.

While all the 13 measures have not been completely implemented in the areas of conflict, there has been a marked reduction in violence from both sides. Points of contention include the city of Mariupol, the capture of which would give the rebels territory close to Crimea.

Conclusion/Workable Solution

For lasting peace, there has to be a candid acknowledgement that there are actually 4 parties to the conflict in Ukraine.

1. Ukraine
2. Russia
3. The Donetsk and Lugansk breakaway republics
4. USA

Ideally the implementation of the Minsk protocol and Minsk II should bring lost lasting peace to southern and eastern Ukraine, but a series of measures guaranteed by the four parties may be the only way out for future conflicts.

Ukraine

For years, the former Soviet republic positioned itself as some sort of a bridge between eastern and western Europe. The 2014 coup and the change in regime has pushed the country towards a completely pro-

West foreign policy, even at the expense of its own citizens in the country's south and east.

A pro-West policy that includes membership of NATO would permanently put Ukraine at odds with Russia, compromising Kiev's own security. While accession to the European Union, which would normally take around 8 to 10 years, is something that the Russian establishment can live with, Ukrainian membership of NATO would be deemed unacceptable by Moscow.

Ukraine needs to declare itself as an independent and neutral state that neither joins NATO nor any future military blocs that Russia may create. In turn, it can request a guarantee of its borders post April 2014 from Russia. It is a mere impossibility for Moscow to surrender Crimea.

Ukraine would also need to guarantee that its own territory would not be used for activities that are inimical to Russian military interests.

It is also essential for the authorities in Kiev to assure Moscow that the rights of Russian-speaking minorities in Ukraine will be respected.

Russia

Russia would be required to guarantee Ukraine's unity and territorial integrity, renouncing any possible future claim on the Ukrainian breakaway republics.

Moscow would also need to ban its servicemen and civilians from participating in any future fighting in Ukraine, making it a criminal offence.

As is the case with Ukraine vis-à-vis Russia, the Russian government would also need to guarantee that its territory would not be used to support insurgents in Ukraine. The Russian state-run television channels have also been accused of fanning the flames of separatism in Ukraine's breakaway republics. This is another area that Moscow should address.

Further, while Russia may be justified in insisting that Ukraine not join NATO, it clearly must state that its neighbor is well within its rights to pursue both closer ties and eventual membership of the European Union (EU).

Considering the fact that some former Warsaw Pact nations that are now members of the EU and are keen on expanding economic, diplomatic and cultural ties with Russia, it would not be inimical to Moscow for Kiev to become a part of the grand European project. Some analysts have even stated from time to time that Ukraine could actually be a bridge between Europe and Russia.

Accepting that a majority of Ukrainians would favor the EU over Vladimir Putin's pet project, the Eurasian Economic Union, would actually help heal some of the wounds between Russia and Ukraine.

Donetsk and Lugansk republics

With a guarantee of autonomy via the Minsk accords, the rebel groups need to accept and implement the accords in letter and spirit and to completely disarm and join the mainstream political process in Ukraine.

USA

The United States would need to guarantee that it would neither call for Ukraine's inclusion into NATO, nor use Ukrainian territory to set up military bases.

With a Russian guarantee of not arming insurgents in Ukraine, the US would need to accept to offer similar guarantees when it comes to training and providing lethal aid to the Ukrainian army. With a guarantee of neutrality fro Ukraine, there is no reason for the country to face any threat either from Russia or its western neighbors with whom it is looking for greater integration.

With the Monroe Doctrine being one of the defining points of US foreign policy, Washington must accept that Moscow has genuine interests and its own sphere of influence in the former Soviet space and Central Asia.

BIBLIOGRAPHY

1. Ukraine death toll hits 6,000 amid ongoing fighting – UN (United Nations Press Service) http://www.un.org/apps/news/story.asp?NewsID=50215#.VT9XQIcxGgQ
2. Alexander Lukin, 'What the Kremlin is Thinking: Putin's Vision for Eurasia', *Foreign Affairs,* July-August 2014. http://www.foreignaffairs.com/articles/141538/alexander-lukin/what-the-kremlin-is-thinking
3. Thomas L. Friedman, 'Why Putin doesn't respect us', *The New York Times,* March 4, 2014. http://www.nytimes.com/2014/03/05/opinion/friedman-why-putin-doesnt-respect-us.html
4. Remarks of Victoria Nuland, Assistant Secretary, Bureau of European and Eurasian Affairs, US Department of State, Washington DC at the *U.S.-Ukraine Foundation Conference,* December 13, 2013. http://www.state.gov/p/eur/rls/rm/2013/dec/218804.htm
5. Odessa erupts into violence again as pro-Russian protesters vent anger against riot police Damien Gayle reports in *The Daily Mail,* 3 May 2014. http://www.dailymail.co.uk/news/article-2619364/Ukraine-braced-bloodshed-Russia-warns-peace-destroyed-violence-east-leaves-dead-violence-spreads-west-Odessa.html
6. Odessa tragedy survivor: 'Many people strangled after escaping the fire'; http://rt.com/news/157256-odessa-witness-massacre-ukraine/
7. Volodymyr Ishchenko, 'Ukraine has ignored the far right too long-it must wake up to the danger', *The Guardian,* 13 November 2014. http://www.theguardian.com/commentisfree/2014/nov/13/ukraine-far-right-fascism-mps
8. According to Donetsk Republic leader, only Russian volunteers fighting with anti-Kiev forces. *RT,* 28 August 2014. http://rt.com/news/183308-russian-volunteers-ukraine-fighting/
9. Patrick Jackson, 'Ukraine War pulls in foreign fighters', *BBC News,* 1 September 2014. http://www.bbc.com/news/world-europe-28951324
10. Gordon Michael and Eric Schmitt, 'U.S. Considers Supplying Arms to Ukraine Forces', *The New York Times,* Feb 1, 2015. http://www.nytimes.com/2015/02/02/world/us-taking-a-fresh-look-at-arming-kiev-forces.html?_r=0
11. Alec Nuhn reports about US paratroopers having begun training Ukraine national guard units, *The Guardian,* 20 April, 2015. http://www.theguardian.com/world/2015/apr/20/us-paratroopers-begin-training-national-guard-units-in-ukraine
12. Petro Poroshenko's tweet on April 20, 2015 https://twitter.com/poroshenko/status/590142933405433858
13. 'Kerry Makes a Case for Russian Complicity in Downing of MH-17', *Reuters,* 7/20/14. http://www.newsweek.com/kerry-makes-case-russian-complicity-downing-mh-17-260006

14. Griff Witte and Karen DeYoung, 'Obama announces expanded sanctions against Russia as E.U. aligns', *The Washington Post,* July 29 2014. http://www.washingtonpost.com/world/europe/europe-agrees-to-sweeping-new-sanctions-against-russia/2014/07/29/97db98e2-e28d-43f8-a2b6-8816f9ce49ec_story.html
15. 'Malaysia Finally on JIT', *New Straits Times,* 12.08.2014; http://www.nst.com.my/node/60321
16. Haris Hussain, 'US analysts conclude MH17 downed by aircraft', *New Straits Times,* 7 August 2014; http://www.nst.com.my/node/20925
17. 'Ukraine: Widespread Use of Cluster Munitions. Government Responsible for Cluster Attacks on Donetsk', *Human Rights Watch,* October 20, 2014; http://www.hrw.org/news/2014/10/20/ukraine-widespread-use-cluster-munitions
18. *Protokol. Po itogom Konsultatsii Trekhstoronnei Kontaktnoi Gruppy Otnositel'no Sovmestnykh Shagov Napravlennykh na Implementatsiyu Mirnovo Plana Presidenta Ukrainy P. Poroshenko i Initsiativ Presidenta Rossii V. Putina* (Minsk Protocol in English); www.osce.org/ru/home/123258?download=true
19. Minsk II Statement (Organisation for Cooperation & Security in Europe); http://www.osce.org/ru/cio/140221?download=true

6

The New Media with Old Content: Reflection of the Ukrainian Conflict in Kyrgyz Segment of Facebook

Asel Murzakulova

Introduction

The conflict in Ukraine has become the most significant recent event in global and regional politics. In general, the conflict potential remains fairly high in the post-Soviet space, and in the early 1990s, conflicts broke out in Tajikistan, Georgia, Azerbaijan and Kyrgyzstan. However, in comparison with other violent events in the CIS, the conflict in Ukraine made a major shift in public opinion, the consequences of which have irrevocably transformed the post-Soviet space into regions with diametrically opposed agendas. In fact, the attitude to the Ukrainian conflict has divided public opinion into two opposing camps. At the same time, it has touched a large layer of the discourse of nationalism that brought about a widespread reflection on estimates of the Soviet past. An important effect that accompanies this conflict since its beginning is an information war unfolded between Russia, Europe and America. The polarization of discourse of controlled media has reached the level of confrontation during the "Cold War" with the familiar methods of information propaganda based on half-truth and sometimes on outright manipulations. It should be noted that in almost all countries of the Central Asian region, the Russian television media is the main channel of access to the world news. Their influence has led to a discussion in some countries about the necessity of their limiting, for example, in Kazakhstan. Sociological studies in different countries of the Central Asian region have shown that television is the main source of information for the majority of the population. Internet is affordable only for a small layer of the population. Despite the fact that quantitatively, the Internet still cannot have full-scale influence on public opinion in the region, the Internet content reflects the vast space for important cultural debates about identity, where the diversity of voices of ordinary citizens shows the most plural picture.

Usually the spread of new media is seen as a raising awareness resource, which is consequently leading to an open and democratic society. The impact of new media in the civil protest actions has been widely discussed after the Arab Spring, experts have repeatedly spoken about the role of Facebook in mobilizing the Egyptian youth. Kyrgyzstan is a country that experienced the so-called "colour revolutions", like Ukraine and Georgia. The focus of the research of these events is usually structural factors like power, economic conditions, the level of criminalization, etc. The impact of the media on civil mobilization in the Kyrgyz revolutions of 2005 and 2010 was not studied. New media were not an object of research and analysis either. It can be argued that the Kyrgyz segment of Facebook remains unexplored. Given the relatively small number of the studies based on information published in the social network, this article aims to throw light on the Facebook discussions with respect to the Ukrainian crisis.

This article studies the Kyrgyz segment of Facebook represented by several groups created in the network by natives of Kyrgyzstan who are not necessarily located in the country at the time of participation in the group. These groups are "Kyrgyzstan Ukraine: dialogue of friendship" (closed group), "Repressed Kyrgyz 1930 (Ukraine)" (Public Group). The group "Kyrgyzstan against the Customs Union" also has a solid proportion of the posts with respect to the studied problem, despite the fact that its thematic focus is different.

Discourse Background: Evaluation by the Foreign Ministry and Experts

The official discourse in the region was presented by statements of the Kyrgyz Foreign Ministry, Kazakh Foreign Ministry and the Foreign Ministry of Uzbekistan, and the overall tone of the statements was similar and contained calls for a speedy settlement of the conflict through negotiations. It should be noted that the Kyrgyz Foreign Ministry published two contradictory statements. In the first statement on March 11, 2014, the Ministry expressed the support for the change of power of Viktor Yanukovych and the greeting of the new authorities in Ukraine. In the second statement, which was published on March 20, 2014, the Ministry of Foreign Affairs of Kyrgyzstan called the results of the referendum on the accession of Crimea to Russia "the will of absolute majority of the population" of the peninsula. At the same time, Kyrgyzstan appealed to Russia and Ukraine and called for "restraint" and peace talks: "Any initiatives and actions should be aimed solely at preserving the fragile peace and stability in Ukraine and in this region as a whole, and the force methods are unacceptable".

The Ukrainian conflict has demonstrated the diversity of assessments and views among experts on how it can affect the countries of Central Asia. Some people point to the fact that the conflict has shown the importance of regional integration projects without the participation of Russia. For example, as noted by the expert F. Tolipov, "The Crimea crisis will have profound geopolitical implications for Central Asia, where the events are understood as the expression of a new rise in Russia's neo-imperialism. Over time, Moscow can repair this image in the eyes of countries and peoples on Russia's perimeter, but one thing has once again become obvious: Central Asians, while attempting to resolve regional issues and construct their common regional home should concentrate on finding regional solutions rather than seeking great power mediation".

According to Slavomír Horák, a peculiarity of the Ukrainian crisis could be the loss of Central Asia as the last Russia-oriented region. Kazakhstan and Turkmenistan, less vulnerable to labour migration, already tend more to look at China. According to the expert, "Finally, while acquiring a relatively small area in Crimea, Russia could pay a high price by losing Central Asia as the last territory willing to be under its influence.[2]

Other influential authors point to the important effects of the crisis in terms of conflict potential available in the region: "The "frozen" conflicts inherited from the collapse of the Soviet Union can become hot again at any moment, especially if Moscow seeks to make it happen under the pretext of protecting minorities or Russian-speaking populations. This raises questions about the future of formerly contested terrain in Central Asia, such as the Uzbek enclaves in Kyrgyzstan, the mostly Russian populated north of Kazakhstan, or the towns of Samarkand and Bukhara in Uzbekistan".[3]

The discourse of threat to Central Asia by Russia appeared in the global media. The well-known analyst Stephen Blank writes in Diplomat that the main conclusion that can be drawn from the Ukrainian crisis is that the lack of a US strategy towards the Central Asian countries and that Russian could at any time plunge them into chaos, if its leadership is challenged by the local elites.[4]

It should be noted that the above estimates were rare in the discussions in social networks, and we can talk about the separate existence of not only the content, but also the discourse on the whole depending on the source. At the same time, if the geopolitical dimension of the conflict remained at the center of discussions among the majority of experts, Facebook groups focused on the discussion of the cultural component of the conflict and its consequences, as will be shown in the next section.

Facebook Discussions about Ukraine

The analysis in this section will be based on the monitoring of debates on the pages of several groups organized by Kyrgyzstani people on Facebook. This monitoring was conducted during 2014-2015. To comply with the ethical issues, names of social network users will not be mentioned. The analysis presented in this section is the result of a generalized monitoring of 3 groups.

The analysis here posits three questions:

- What are the effects produced by facebook discussions about the Ukrainian crisis?
- How is the concept of "historical destiny" argued?
- Despite the isolation of the discussion content on television and radio, is there an inverse relationship between "traditional" and new sources?

During the period of high conflict escalation, the content of publications on Facebook looked like a battlefield. Each event in eastern Ukraine was followed by sharp reaction on Facebook. If the first posts and publications were around the question "what is happening?", soon they turned into a question "Who is guilty?".

This is perhaps the central issue of discussion that divided users into multiple camps. One of the important effects of the discussions was the emergence of identities: people supporting Russia's position in the conflict, as well as positively assessing the Soviet past, were called "*vatniki*".[5]

It should be noted that if in the initial phase of the conflict, discussions in the studied groups were sharp and represented diametrically opposed opinions, the separation between the parties on the basis of selection of opinion occurred rather quickly. Publications of "lists" of *vatniki* and Westerners (supporters of Maidan and of the new government of Ukraine) began to appear in both public and private groups.

It should be noted that in Facebook discussions, the user's position on the conflict tended to coincide with his/her assessment of the Soviet past. In this respect, it is important to say that the conflict in Ukraine was considered in a different plane than the Russian-Georgian conflict in 2008. The idea of "Slavic brotherhood, present in the Soviet period and developed into the concept of "Russian World", was based on the special closeness of Russia and Ukraine. On the one hand, it worked as a distance in the estimates of the conflict through the prism of the common heritage; therefore, the conflict was presented by a "motive" of betrayal. On the other hand, it was seen as "the determination of one's own way." Another important effect was the actualization of the common intersections in the "fates" of Central Asian and Ukrainian societies. For the studied discussions, there are several intersections of "historical destiny", on the basis of which there was formed the discourse of solidarity with Ukraine. First, the repressions of the 1930s, when a large part of the repressed "enemies of the people" were deported from the territory of modern Kyrgyzstan to Ukraine. Secondly, there are many common things in the revolutionary period of independence.

The main narrative of the conflict was understood in terms of violation of the golden rule – the evaluation of the Soviet past was supposed to be consonant with the Russian one. Too much independence in this sense is a direct path to a conflict with Russia. Despite the polarity and sometimes open conflict between users of the social network, the discussions showed **the need to learn more alternative information**.

The discussions in the network were often built on the denial or discussion of the formal television content.

Each information related to say, execution of the wife or child of a pro-Russian militant of a pro-Russian militant[6] quickly raised doubt, denial or support on Facebook. This indicates that many Facebook users also proved to be attentive audience of TV channels. Screenshots from the news releases of the first TV channel became popular themes, around which the discussion unfolded. The popularization of the

Ukrainian mass media in the studied segment also attracts attention. Links and posts with reports and stories from Ukrainian media have become a kind of strategy to find a balance in the information war. Against the background of the increasing polarization of the discourse, Bektur Iskender, a famous user of social networks and the founder of the famous Kyrgyz news website Kloop, made several trips to Ukraine, organized by the funds collected on the network. From his field trips, Bektur Iskender aimed to reflect on an alternative situation in Ukraine. This, to the Central Asian Facebook user, was different as the general opinion was that antagonism prevailed among the Russian, Ukrainian and western media.

Conclusion

If we ask how Facebook discussions reflect the views of the majority and how they can serve as a slice of public opinion, we can say that from the standpoint of coverage, they remain a marginalized segment of the formation of public opinion and cannot fully compete with traditional TV and radio. However, in terms of the reflection of plurality of existing opinions without editorial policy of Facebook, they could be a productive subject of study.

Obviously, the control of content on Facebook is highly conditional and virtually absent, allowing one to see the variety of opinions, not to analyze the given information agenda as it happens during the analysis of television content. We can fully support the statement of the reflectivity of this information segment.

Also interesting is the effect that the emergence of manipulators in the form of "trolls" has also found opposition among the participants through the re-publication of statuses and posts in the form of argument.

Largely, the Ukrainian conflict is not perceived as an external conflict by facebook users, but as a showdown within a common space, hence there is extrapolation of these events on one's own past (such as the famine in Ukraine and Kazakhstan, crimes of collectivization and others).

One of the significant consequences has been the emergence of common agenda between the Kyrgyz, Russian, Kazakh, Ukrainian and international segment of *Facebook*.

ENDNOTES

1. Farkhod Tolipov, Ukraine and the CIS Perspective: Implications for Central Asia, CACI Analyst, 04/04/2014. http://www.cacianalyst.org/publications/analytical-articles/item/12949-ukraine-and-the-cis-perspective-implications-for-central-asia.html
2. Slavomír Horák Russia's Intervention in Ukraine Reverberates in Central Asia, CACI Analyst, 03/19/2014. http://www.cacianalyst.org/publications/analytical-articles/item/12935-russias-intervention-in-ukraine-reverberates-in-central-asia.html
3. Marlene Laruelle and Sean Roberts Why Ukraine's crisis keeps central Asian leaders up at night, *Washington Post*, March 7, 2014. http://www.washington post.com/blogs/monkey-cage/wp/2014/03/07/why-ukraines-crisis-keeps-central-asian-leaders-up-at-night/
4. What Crimea Teaches Central Asia, *The Diplomat*, May 27, 2014. http://thediplomat.com/2014/05/what-crimea-teaches-central-asia/
5. "vatniki" - quilted jackets - derived from the name of the warm winter clothing that was widespread in labor camps and labor collectives in the USSR.
6. A refugee from Slaviansk recalls how the wife and a youn son of a militant was executed, Official site of the first channel. http://www.1tv.ru/news/world/262978

Index